MOSES:
ISRAEL'S GREAT LEADER

From Egypt to Canaan was a few days' journey . . .
Why did it take forty years?
Why did only two that left Egypt enter Canaan?

MOSES:
ISRAEL'S GREAT LEADER

REV. DR. MARION TRIPP

Author of an unusual book:

"What Was God Doing Before He Made Man?"

and

Other Biblical Works

Library of Congress Control Number:		2011906583
ISBN:	Hardcover	978-1-4628-6385-3
	Softcover	978-1-4628-6384-6
	Ebook	978-1-4628-6386-0

This book was printed in the United States of America.

To order additional copies of this book, contact:
Xlibris Corporation
1-888-795-4274
www.Xlibris.com
Orders@Xlibris.com
94156

CONTENTS

Chapter Nine

Chapter Ten

Chapter Eleven

Chapter Twelve

Charts

This book is

dedicated

To my three grandchildren

Tracy Tripp

Thomas Tripp

Tiffany Tripp

A NOTE FROM THE AUTHOR

One often ponders upon reading a good book, some thinking, what an alternate title might have been. Some books are to be just tasted or savored and some to be digested. This one is definitely in the later category.

One chapter at a time, it is ideal for personal Bible study groups, for youth groups, Bible study groups in homes or church. It is thoroughly Biblical.

Moses. Israel's great leader, leaving Egypt for Canaan could have been just a few days journey. Why did it take forty years? Why did only two that left Egypt enter Canaan?

Also, herein, is a study of the "Ten Commandments" and "The structure of the Tabernacle," which is one of the great type and shadows of Jesus Christ, who was to come.

May you, the reader, be blessed as you study from chapter to chapter.

INTRODUCTION

Moses was of the tribe of Levi. He was the son of Amram and Jochebed. His mother was the granddaughter of Jacob (Israel). He had an elder sister, Miriam, and an elder brother, Aaron. His birth was about 1350 BC. His life is divided into three forty-year periods;

Forty years in Pharaoh's court;
Forty years in Midian;
Forty years leading the Israelites.

This study is compiled to bring forth anointment, easy to read, and understanding.

All scripture quotes are from the original King James translation, and the spelling is as it appears in the text.

May God bless you, the reader, as you read and study the content.

CHAPTER ONE

Period of Beginnings

The first eleven chapters of Genesis cover a period from the time of the restoration of the earth of the time of Abraham. This period is concerned with beginnings. The Genesis account tells of the restoration of the earth, is climaxed with the creation of man, and the institution of the home, and the Sabbath, and then followed by the temptation and the fall of man, with the consequent punishment. This is followed by the account of Cain slaying Abel and the birth of Seth. Very little is said about mankind during this period, with the exception of Enoch, who is said to have walked with God. God took him; this is the first rapture recorded in the scripture.

Then, in the days of Noah, we have the account of the wickedness of man, the building of the ark, the universal flood that destroyed all of mankind, with the exception of Noah and his family.

After the flood, God begins the human race all over again with Noah, his wife, his three sons, and their wives. This is followed by the building of the Tower of Babel, the confusion of the language, and the scattering of the people over the face of the earth.

The Second Period begins with Abraham and goes to the time of Moses. This history is recorded in Genesis beginning with chapter twelve and goes through chapter fifty. The content of this period may be summarized as follows:

The call of Abraham and his accomplishments;
The experience of his son Isaac.
The life of Jacob and his name changed to Israel; his sons who became the twelve tribes of Israel.
The struggle and achievements of Joseph in Egypt.

Finally, the account of Israel and his family of seventy coming to Egypt and given the land of Goshen.

At the age of 147, Israel comes to the end of his days. His death brought no change to the status of the Israelites in Egypt. Joseph quieted any of their fears with the assurance of his goodwill, and the Egyptians did them no harm.

At the age of 110, Joseph called his brothers about his bed and reminded them that in due time, they would return to Canaan, and he also secured the promise that they would take his body to the homeland with them and bury him there with his forefathers.

As long as Joseph, who occupied such prominent place in the government affairs, was alive, the Israelites were in favored position. They had homes, employment, and were cordially accepted by the Egyptians. But, after the death of Joseph, there soon arose a new king over Egypt who knew not Joseph. This new ruler inaugurated a new policy toward the Israelites. They became to be regarded as foreigners and slaves. Because of their rapid increase in the numbers, they were feared as a threat to the security of the government. The new Pharaoh set cruel task makers over them, forcing them to do the hardest kind of work—that of making brick.

Now, the sons of Israel were no longer a free people. They were now slaves; their life was now one of oppression and suffering. But, despite the cruel treatment placed upon them, they continued to multiply. The Pharaoh now gives orders to the midwives to kill all male babies born to the Israelites. The midwives refused to carry out the orders.

The Pharaoh issued a desperate command. "Every male son born to the Israelites shall be cast into the Nile river." There is no way of knowing how many babies were destroyed in this manner. We do know one was not, that one being Moses.

CHAPTER TWO

Moses Is Born

Moses is born into a family of faith. Amram, a member of the Levite tribe, married a cousin from the same tribe, whose name was Jochebed, a granddaughter of Israel, to whom was born three children, Miriam, Aaron, and Moses. These children, who were to figure so prominently in the history of their people, were given a good start in life by having a godly mother and father.

The name Jochebed means "Jehovah Thy Glory." In the midst of affliction, she rejoiced that she could trust God. She determined that she would serve God at all cost.

When Moses was born, his mother, Jochebed, was able to hide him away for three months. The time came when bold steps had to be taken. Everything must be risked on faith in God. Jochebed made a basket, placed the child in it, and placed him in the reeds of the shallows of the Nile River. Miriam, his sister, stood afar watching to see what would take place.

Adopted by Pharaoh's Daughter

Pharaoh's daughter came with her handmaiden to bathe, found the baby-filled basket, and took him as her own. Miriam was ready with the suggestion for a nurse. What a risk was taken?! What if Pharaoh's daughter had failed to take a kindly interest in the child and had turned him over to the guards? Not only would the child have been destroyed, but, in all probability, the parents would have been killed also. Jochebed had faith, and that turned her risk into a glorious venture that she believed would somehow turn out well.

Now see how the hand of God worked. The very thing that was to destroy him saved him. Miriam was ready with the suggestion of a nurse and was asked to secure one. Miriam brings Jochebed, the child's birth mother for the nurse.

Exodus 2:9: Pharaoh's daughter gives Jochebed instruction: ". . . take the child away and nurse it for me, I will give thee thy wage."

Not only was her son saved, but she would receive compensation in addition. She was not trying to make money, was just trying to save her child. God gave the child to her and also a measure of material blessing. Jesus promised the sams principle when he said, "Seek ye first the kingdom of God and his righteousness, and all these things shall be added unto you" (Matt. 6:23).

So, in his formative years, the child was cared for by his birth mother. When he was weaned, she brought him unto Pharaoh's daughter. She called his name Moses, because she drew him out of the water (Exod. 2:10).

What a story of faith! Jochebed gave her best to the child in training him in his tender years. When it came time, she gave him up to become the son of another, because it was God's will and for the highest good for the child.

In Pharaoh's court, he would have the best advantage in all the land. He would receive education and culture there that he could not possible get elsewhere. God was preparing him for what he would need in later years.

It is thoroughly likely that Jochebed continued to be his nurse after she presented him to Pharaoh's daughter for he would be with his adopted mother a short while each day. He would have been with his teacher and nurse a much longer period of time. The nurse had the privilege of putting him to bed, attending to his clothing, and seeing that he was presentable when the princess called for him.

Fading more and more into the background, Jochebed was comforted as she saw her son receive the highest privileges in the land. In the time that he was with her, as she changed his clothes, bathed him, tucked into bed, she no doubt told him the stories of Israel's past, and what Jehovah God must have in store for the Israelites.

Scripture gives little detail of his boyhood. A tale of his early childhood is told in "Jewish Talmud," which is the work that embodies the "Canonical and Law of the Jews." It contains those rules, precepts, and interpretation by which the Jewish people confessed to be their guide. A story goes:

One day when Moses was three years old, he snatched the crown from the Pharaoh's head and placed it on his head. Pharaoh devised a test to see if he was aware of his transgression. Two plates were set before the child.

One was filled with gold, and the other with red hot coals. If the child chose the gold, death would be the reward. If he chose the coals, he should be spared as one without knowledge of his act. Moses took the coals and put them to his mouth and tongue. His life was spared. Henceforth, he would be haltering in speech.

In light of the Scripture, Moses was schooled in the Egyptian school system, which was highly developed. Acts 7:22: "And Moses was learned in all the wisdom of the Egyptians and was mighty in word and deed."

During his period of schooling, he may have had classmates as far away as the Euphrates River. He would have learned quite a bit about geography and history. Egyptian learning at the middle of the second millennium BC was at a high level. It is not much to imagine that as the son of Pharaoh's daughter he would have been given the best available to the royal family.

We can be certain that in the first years of his life, his birth mother, Jochebed, would acquaint him with God's plan for the Hebrew people; she surely would have told him the stories of Abraham, Isaac, Jacob, and Joseph.

At some point in his life, he became aware that he was not Egyptian, that he was an Israelite. He grew increasingly resentful of the way in which the Egyptians treated the Israelites. We have no way of knowing the struggle that must have gone on in his mind during these years. As the son of Pharaoh's daughter, he might succeed to the throne some day. Should he forget his oppressed people, seek fame and office among the people who adopted him? We find the answer from scripture, Hebrews 11:24-25: "By Faith, Moses when he had come to years, refused to be called the son of Pharaoh's daughter. Choosing rather to suffer with his people of God, than to enjoy the pleasures of sin for a season."

One day, seeing an Egyptian beating a Hebrew, one of his fellow men, he took matters into his hands. He killed the Egyptian and buried him in the sand. He could have thought this act would cause them to accept him as their deliverer and support him. The very next day, when he saw two Hebrew fighting, he asked, "Wherefore smitest thy brother?"

Their answer, "Who made thee prince and judge over us, intend thou to kill me, as thou killed the Egyptian?"

Now Moses fears saying, "Surely this thing is known." When Pharaoh learned of it, he sought to kill Moses. Moses flees, goest to Midian, where he will spend the next forty years.

CHAPTER THREE

Moses in Midian

When Moses reached Midian, he found a well of water. Here he sits. One cannot help to wonder what was he thinking as he sits there.

The priest of Midian had seven daughters. They were tending their fathers flock and came to the well to water them. Other sheepherders came driving them away. Moses stands up, and comes to their aid, drives them away, and drew water for their flock. When they returned home, their father asks why they were home so early. They say, "An Egyptian delivered us out of the hands of the shepherds, and also drew enough for us and our flock" (Exod. 2:19).

Their father asks, "Where is he? Why is it that ye have left the man? Call him, that he may eat bread."

Moses was content to dwell with them. I suppose if you were alone with no one, no home, no job, no anything, it would be a relief to have a home. But, the fact is, God was working in the life of Moses. He will now spend forty years here in Midian. Reuel, the priest, gave Moses one of his daughters, Zepporah, for a wife. She bares Moses two sons.

Here in Midian, he will live a quite life of a shepherd for forty years. He would have time to mediate on the things taught him by his birth mother and digest the things learned in Egypt. Also, would learn the ways of desert tribes. The hand of God can be seen in this period of his life. God was preparing him for the great task that was yet before him.

The Burning Bush (Exod. 3:1-13)

While on the backside of the desert, tending his father-in-law's flocks, suddenly, a bush is burning, but it is not being consumed. Moses turns aside to see why it was not being consumed. When the Lord saw that he had turned aside to see, he called unto him out of the burning bush, "Moses, Moses."

Moses says, "Here am I"

God gives him instruction, "Draw not nigh, put off thy shoes, the ground were you stand is holy ground." Then, God identifies himself as the God of Abraham, Isaac, and Jacob, tells him that he has heard the cries of his people back in Egypt, and is now ready to deliver them. He will bring them out of bondage into a land that flows with milk and honey, into a place of the Canaanite, Hittites, Amorites, Perizzites, Hivites, and Jebusites. Then says to him, "come now thee therefore, and I will send thee to Pharaoh, that thou mayest bring forth my people the children of Israel out of Egypt" (Exod. 3:10).

Moses asks, "Who am I, that I should go back unto Pharaoh and that I should bring forth the children of Israel out of Egypt?" (Exod. 3:11).

God answers in verse 12, "Certainly, I will be with thee, and this shall be a token unto thee, that I have sent thee; when thou hast brought forth the people out of Egypt, they shall serve God upon the mountain."

Moses is now eighty years old and knows the will of God for his life. Knows now is the time to do it. So, what will he do?

Exodus 3:13-15: "And Moses said unto God, behold, when I come unto the children of Israel, and shall say unto them, The God of your fathers hath sent me unto you; and they shall say unto me, What is thy name? what shall I say unto them? And God said unto Moses, I AM THAT I AM; and he said, Thus shalt thou say unto the children of Israel, I AM hath sent me unto you. And God said moreover unto Moses, Thus shalt thou say unto the children of Israel, the Lord God of you fathers, the God of Abraham, the God of Isaac, and the God of Jacob, hath sent me unto you: this is my memorial unto all generations."

Then, Moses makes a second excuse, Exodus 4:10: ". . . O my Lord, I am not eloquent, I am slow of speech. And slow of tongue. (remember the story of the red hot coals he put to his mouth and tongue when he was three years old.) God offers to heal him, but he refuses. He thought it best that he have a spoke person. This angered God, but he gave him his request. Aaron would be his spoke person.

Jethro, his father-in-law, gave his consent for him to return to Egypt. So off he goes, armed with the promise that Jehovah that he would be with him.

Chapter Four

Moses Returns to Egypt

Exodus 4:19-20: "And the Lord said unto Moses in Midian, Go, return to Egypt, for all the men are dead which sought your life. And Moses took his wife and his sons, and set them upon an ass, and he returned to the land of Egypt, and Moses took the rod of God in his hand."

If Moses entertained any notion of an early, easy victory, he was sure in for a great surprise. He was fully aware of the difficulties he must meet in his new undertaking. Certainly, he knew some of them, but mercifully not all of them. One of the greatest obstacles was that of persuading the Israelites themselves. He must lead them to understand they could and should leave Egypt. For over four hundred years, they were in Egypt. They had lost consciousness of their mission as a race. For long years, they had been slaves. The confidence in themselves had long been destroyed by their years of slavery. They were defeated and demoralized. Moses must build up their moral, must persuade them they could and must leave Egypt. Then too, the Egyptians had no intention of letting six hundred thousand slaves get beyond their control. For sure, they would not willingly surrender this vast number.

Aaron Joins Moses

The Lord spoke to Aaron, "Go into the wilderness and meet Moses." When he met him, Moses tells him all the words that God had spoke to him. *So off they go!*

When they meet Pharaoh, they were haughtily refused and sent away. At the same time, Pharaoh issued a decree by requiring the Israelites to find their own straw for making the bricks, but still required them to make the same number as before. This burdened the Israelites even more.

God Prepares Moses for the Ordeal Ahead

God lets Moses know that Pharaoh will be stubborn, but victory would be achieved only after a long struggle. That victory will be achieved only by the power of Jehovah.

Now the struggle begins between God of the Hebrew and the gods of the Egyptians. When Aaron cast his rod on the ground, it turned into a snake. Pharaoh sent for his magicians. They came, cast their rods on the ground, and they also turned into snakes. At that point, it seemed that the contest was over. But, Aaron's rod-snake crawled over and swallowed all of the magicians' rod-snakes. This was an indication that the worship of Jehovah, as represented by Moses, was superior to the gods of Egypt. Pharaoh dismissed it as a show and refused to listen.

Now Comes the Plagues

It is well to note that each succeeding plague became more and more severe than the former one, climaxing with the death of the first born of Egypt. The order of the plagues are as follows:

1. Water turned to blood;
2. Frogs cover the land;
3. Lice through the land;
4. Swarms of flies;
5. Murrain of the cattle;
6. Boils on men and beast;
7. A grievous hail;
8. The locust came;
9. Darkness came over the land;
10. Death of the first born;

The final blow was the death of the first born of Egypt. This proved to them that Jehovah is the only true God. The visit of the death angel to every Egyptian home, including Pharaoh's, showed that Jehovah alone exercised control over life and proved the weakness of the Egyptian gods.

For the death angel to pass over the Israelite home, they were to select a lamb on the tenth day of the month, sacrifice it on the fourteenth day, and sprinkle the blood on the two sides of the door post and the upper door post. "When I see the blood, I will pass over you, and the plague shall not be upon you to destroy you, when I smite the land of Egypt" (Exod. 12:13).

Now, look back at Exodus 12:1-5:

1. And the Lord spake unto Moses and Aaron in the land of Egypt, saying,
2. This month shall be unto you the beginning of months, it shall be the first month of the year for you.
3. Speak unto the congregation of Israel, saying, in the tenth day of the month they shall take every man a lamb for a house.
4. And if the household be too little for the lamb, let him and his neighbor next unto his house take according to the number of souls: every man according to his eating shall take it out from sheep, or from the goats.

The lamb was singled out from the herd, separated, appointed to death four days before it was slain.

See here the type and shadow of Jesus Christ. Isaiah 53:7:

"Brought as a lamb before the slaughter."

John the baptizer called out four years before Jesus was crucified. "Behold the lamb of God that taketh away the sin of the world."

Now look back at Exodus the twelfth chapter:

Verse 3----------------------*It Is "A Lamb"*
Verse 4----------------------*It Is "The Lamb"*
Verse 5 ---------------------*It Is "Your Lamb"*

The order is most instructive. While in sin, before *the new birth*, Jesus is nothing more than *a lamb*. We saw him, but there was no beauty that we should desire him. When the Spirit of God awaken our spirit, caused us to see our sinful condition, turning our gaze toward Jesus, then we beheld him as *the Lamb* finally. When one repents, believes, Jesus becomes *your Lamb*.

Isaiah 53:5: "He was wounded for our transgressions, he was bruised for our iniquities, the chastisement of our peace was upon him; and with his stripes we are healed." "To make it personal, Jesus was wounded for my transgressions, Jesus was bruised for my iniquities, the chastisement of my peace was upon Jesus, and with the stripes of Jesus, I am healed."

Back to the plagues . . . The midnight cry

At midnight, a cry went up from the land of Egypt; a cry that began with the first discovered dead child, followed by family after family of the Egyptians learned its sorrow, until the whole nation travailed in grief, including Pharaoh.

Only the Israelites were not weeping. The death angel had passed over their houses because of the blood on the door post.

The Israelites were dressed, packed, and ready to leave Egypt. Waiting for the break of day, for they had been instructed not to leave their house before day (Exod. 12:22).

When Israel and his family went into Egypt, their number was seventy-seventy. Now leaving Egypt, some four hundred and fifty years later, six hundred thousand men above twenty years of age were leaving. Counting the women, children, and very old, the entire multitude numbered approximately two million. Also, there was a mixed multitude went with them. They were Egyptians.

The Egyptians were so eager for them to leave that they were willing to give them anything they ask for. They just wanted them to be gone. So as the Israelites left Egypt, they had flocks, herds, much cattle. They had fine clothing, jewels, and many other gifts. They went out a rich people. God had enriched them that they may have to give back to him for the building of the Tabernacle.

CHAPTER FIVE

Leaving Egypt

The Family Becomes a State

When the Israelites went out of Egypt, God connected with them only through his covenant with Abraham, bringing them to himself nationally. Put them under the Mosaic Covenant. Moses was the first mediator over the nation of Israel. As Jesus Christ is the mediator between God and man today, Moses was for Israel. In the commandments, God taught Israel his just demands, convicted them of sin, provided a priesthood and sacrifice, gave guilty people a way of forgiveness, and restoration to fellowship and worship.

Left Egypt in Order

Despite the great number, when the Israelites went out of Egypt, they were well organized. Exodus 13:18: ". . . and The children of Israel went up harnessed out of the land of Egypt." The word "harnessed" here means, "rank upon rank" or "file upon file." They left in a military formation. Every one knew their place. Their prayers had been answered. The days of bondage was over. They were now on their way to the *Promised Land*, but many hard days would be ahead of them.

The shortest route from Egypt to Canaan would have been in the northeasterly direction, along the Mediterranean. This familiar route was followed by most of the people traveling. It is only natural that we ask, why did they not take this route? They could have been there in days. *Reason being* God was to provide a specific course of preparation to their mission as a nation. They were not to go immediately to the *Promised Land. Why?* Because there was to be a period of special instruction. They had to be led to Mt. Sinai. There, "*the Law*" would be given to them.

They would be given instruction in every detail of the Law by which every phase of their lives was to be regulated. There a Tabernacle was to be built, which would teach them how to approach God.

Route Taken

Exodus 13:18: "God led the people out, through the way of the wilderness of the Red Sea."

Their first resting place was at Succoth, then on to Etham, in the edge of the wilderness. Here, God gave them a symbol of his presence; a pillar of a cloud by day, a pillar of fire by night. They were not lead around the north end of the Red Sea, but were commanded to camp at Pihahiroth with the Red Sea in front of them.

Crossing the Red Sea

A lookout sees a cloud of dust out on the horizon. Senses that it is Pharaoh. For sure it was. God had hardened his heart and now he was on his way after them. God had said he would do this. (See chapter fourteen of Exodus.) The lookout rushed to Moses, shouting that the Egyptians were coming. The people became excited as the news spread throughout the camp; they thought they were trapped. All they could see, here they are between the sea and the desert, with the Egyptians riding hard upon them from the rear. What could they do? Moses was not overwhelmed; he was a man of prayer. He knew that they were there because God had led them there. He says to the people, "Fear not, stand still, and see the salvation of the Lord, which he will show you today: for the Egyptians whom ye have seen today, ye shall see them again no more for ever. The Lord shall fight for you, and ye shall hold your peace" (Exod. 14:13-14).

God was getting ready to make a demonstration before them of his supremacy over the gods of the Egyptians. Therefore, they should never be able to doubt his willingness and power to take care of them in any experience that may come their way. An angel of the Lord went before the camp, removed, and went behind them. The pillar of the cloud went from their face and stood behind them; came between the Egyptians and their camp was a cloud of darkness to the Egyptians, but to the Israelite gave light by night to see so that one came not near all night.

Moses stretched out his hand over the sea, and the Lord caused a mighty wind making a path through the sea bed. The next morning they marched over on dry ground. The waters were a great wall unto them on their left and on their right.

When all were safe on the other side, God lifted the cloud. And the Egyptians saw the Israelites had left their camp and crossed the sea on dry ground. Confident, they could do anything the Israelites could, Pharaoh's force drove into the bed of the sea. God caused the wind to change, and the walls of water came in. The heavy chariots began to sink. The mighty army, the horses, all were destroyed by the water. The Israelites saw the Egyptian's dead bodies upon the sea shore. They recognized this as the deliverance of God. Moses expressed his gratitude in a son of victory in Exodus 15:1-18. Miriam took timbrel in hand and began to dance. All the other women joined in with her.

As they turned away from the sea, they must have experienced a new feeling of security. In a brief span of the night, they had been delivered from the danger of the Egyptians once and for all.

Now stretched before them were the lower plains of the Arabian Desert. There was no need to hurry. With the Egyptians out of the way, they could proceed leisurely, allowing the animals to graze.

Survival in the Desert

From the Red Sea, Moses leads the people southward into the Sinai wilderness of Shur—a barren, waterless desert. An occasional tamarisk tree or acacia bush were about the only plants able to survive in the hostile climate. Each night, they shivered in their tents, for the scorching heat of the day disappeared with the setting of the sun, and the temperature dropped greatly.

After three days, without finding water, they came to Marah. Here was plenty of water, but it was bitter and undrinkable. The people complained to Moses, "What shall we drink?" Moses quickly remedied the situation. He took a small tamarisk tree, threw it into the water, and the water became sweet. They and their flocks drank their fill. They filled their goat-skin bags and continued their journey southward until they reached the oasis of Elim. Here they pitched their tents and rested for several weeks, enjoying the twelve wells of water, and the seventy palm trees.

Refreshed by their stay at Elim, they set across the vast wilderness of Sinai toward the Sinai mountain. After several days, the people begin to complain of hunger. Remembering the plenteous vegetables and meats they enjoyed back in Egypt. They groaned, "Would that we had died in the land of Egypt. When we sat by the flesh pots and ate bread to the full. For you have brought us out into this wilderness to kill this whole assembly with hunger."

God again meets their need. In the morning, they were given manna—a bread-like substance which cams like dew on the ground. Every morning, it came with exception of the Sabbath.

From Elim they go to Rephidim, but there was no water there for them to drink. To their habit, they complained against Moses, blaming him for their hardship. In vain, Moses reminded them that Jehovah was still their God, that they were tempting him. That only added to their anger. They became so excited that they were ready to stone Moses. Moses cries out to God, "What shall I do?"

God's answer in Exodus 17:6: "Behold, I will stand before thee upon the rock of Horeb; and thou shalt smite the rock, and there shall come forth water out of it, that the people may drink." Moses did so, and water came forth.

Their First Military Battle

The Amalekites were their next problem. They challenged their right to pass through their country. The Amalekites were an old nation. We have reference to them as a nation in the early life of Abraham.

Now the Israelites had to defend themselves in battle. Moses had discovered that Joshua was a courageous and capable leader. Moses had given him the task of selecting and training an army. Now he is to lead them against the enemy. Moses, Aaron, and Hur stood on top of a hill. Moses stretched forth his hands, holding the rod that had been symbolic of God's presence. As long as Moses held up his hands, Israel prevailed. When he let down his hands, Amalek prevailed. When Moses could no longer hold up his hands, Aaron on one side and Hur on the other side held up Moses hands. Joshua won the battle. Now they came to the wilderness of Sanai. The report of their presence in the vicinity and the victory over Amalek was brought to Jethro—Moses's father-in-law. Jethro comes with Moses's wife and two sons. Evidently, Moses has sent his wife and sons back to Midian after starting to Egypt.

As they approached the camp, Moses went out to meet them and brought them to his tent. They make themselves comfortable as Moses recounted his experience since leaving Midian, dwelling at length on the miraculous way which Jehovah had delivered his people again and again, apparently. Jethro believed in Jehovah, for he rejoiced with his son-in-law. He joined him in a special sacrifice of thanksgiving. Then came the leaders of Israel to welcome Jethro with a feast.

Jethro, seeing how Moses time was taken up in judging matters of the people, suggested that he appoint judges who were able men that feared God. He suggested that Moses reach them the ordinances and laws, and let them rule over small groups in small matters. Every great matter would be brought to Moses. This Moses agreed to. Jethro leaves and returns to his homeland.

CHAPTER SIX

They Come to Mt. Sinai

Exodus 19:1: "The third month when the children of Israel were gone out of the land of Egypt, the same day came they unto the wilderness of Sinai."

Here marks the beginning of the fifth dispensation of time. *The dispensation of Law* begins in Exodus 19:8, and goes to the cross, Matthew 27:35.

There have been four dispensation of time before this dispensation.

> *Innocency . . .*
> *Conscience . . .*
>   *Government . . .*
>   *Promise . . .*
>   *Now, the Law . . .*

There will be two more after *the Law.*

Grace, the church age . . . And the millennium . . . After the millennium, time will be no more . . .

Question: Was God so fickle-minded that he must change his mind seven times? *That is not the case.* Even though there are seven dispensations, they are one in principle. Each dispensation requires more and more of man. Before God made man, he planed the dispensations. His plan for man is progressive.

Each dispensation is a period of time in which man is tested in respect of obedience to a specific revelation of the will of God for man. God simply lets man know what he expects of him during that period of time.

Let us now see how God will deal with his people during this dispensation.

How the Law Was Communicated

God first spoke the Law, then wrote the Ten Commandments on two tablets of stone. Moses broke them; Moses had to hew two tablets of stone and take them upon the mountain, and God wrote them a second time.

Preparation for the Law

Before the delivery of the Law here at Sinai, the people were prepared by special commandment. For three days, they were to purify themselves. Then they were to be led by Moses to the lower part of the mountain. Here they were to remain. Under no condition were they to touch the mountain. The Lord came in a flame of fire, in a loud voice proclaimed the "Ten Commandments" to all the people. This frightened the people, and they insisted that Moses alone talk to God.

Moses went up into the mountain alone. God, with his finger, wrote the commandments on two tablets of stone. While Moses was here in the mountain, God also gave him instruction for the Tabernacle and the Ark of the Covenant.

The long and detailed list of laws are divided into three divisions.

The Moral Law: Which is briefly stated in the Ten Commandments.

The Ceremonial Law: Containing all the details for worship and service, such as, the priesthood, holy season, and many other such matters. Every phase of the religious life of this new Israelite nation, whose unique mission was a religious one, was provided for in these detailed instructions.

The Judicial Law: Had to do with civil law, involving such matters as property, administration, justice, court procedures, and so on.

The giving of the law marks not only the most important event in the history of the Hebrew people, but one of the most important in all history. It would be impossible to estimate the importance of the law in human history. For the Israelite, it was of the uttermost significance. For them it was the absolute *Word of God* forever to be observed.

The Moral Law: The Ten Commandments should be considered since these are applied to all people of all time. All ten are carried over into the New Testament. The only change is the Sabbath. Each deal with man's relationship with God and man. These are God's moral laws defining our duty to God and man. They are timeless and unchanging, with the exception of the Sabbath. All through the scripture they are emphasized as the heart of man's obligation

to God and man. No civilized nation could exist without these laws as a basic of its life.

Moses is up in the mountain, away from the people for forty days. In his absence, the people did an almost unthinkable thing. In not knowing what has happened to Moses, they go to Aaron saying, "Make us a god" *Unfortunately,* he yielded to their request. They brought their earrings, bracelets, and other pieces of gold, from which Aaron mold a God in the form of a calf.

Aaron built an altar in front of the calf. Then in a three-day festival, the people offered sacrifice before the golden calf. This showed how deeply the people had been affected by idolatry in Egypt.

To commit such an act at any time would have been a gross sin, but to be guilty of idolatry at the very place where the commandment against idols had been given made the sin double grievous.

Exodus 32:7: "The Lord said to Moses. Go, get thee down; for my people, which thou brought out of the land of Egypt have corrupted themselves."

Verse 19: "And it came to pass, as soon as he came nigh, unto the camp, that he saw the calf, and dancing: Moses's anger waxed hot, he cast the tablets out of his hand, brake them . . ." Then in verse 20, "he took the calf, burned it in the fire, ground it into powder, stirred it into water, and made them drank it."

When Moses saw the people naked, he said, "Who is on the Lord's side let him come unto me." All the sons of Levi gathered unto Moses standing at the gate. Moses says to them, "Put every man his sword by his side, go out from the gate, throughout the camp, slay every man, his brother every man, and his companion." They did as instructed. Three thousand were slain (Exod. 32:25-28).

Now God instructs Moses to hew two tablets of stone and bring them up into the mountain. God, again, with his finger, writes the Ten Commandments on the two tablets.

Up until this point, God saw their need, heard their cries, sent one to lead them, fed them in the wilderness, supplied them with water, and brought them to Sinai.

Now here at Sinai, God will give them simple instruction as to what he demands of them—"*a Law*"; in Hebrew, "*tora*"; the root meaning, "to throw" "point out," which simply means "human direction."

CHAPTER SEVEN

The Ten Commandments

The Written Law: After Moses broke the tablets of the Law, Exodus 34:1, God instructs Moses to hew two tablets of stone and take them up in the mountain. There he will once again write them.

These *Ten Commandments* are carried over into the New Testament, and are timeless and unchanging, with the exception of the Sabbath. Let us take a look at the:

1. *Thou Shalt Have No Other Gods Before Me:*

God's purpose for Israel was that they be a witness to the pagan world, of the reality of the one true God. To do this, they had to be a committed people, whose faith would reject all other gods. So, God gives them a list of guidelines to live by, heading this list was the commandment, "Thou Shalt Have No Other Gods Before Me." God never intended that this rule should ever be changed; it was never to be discarded. It was for all people of all time. Jesus, in his encounter with Satan in the wilderness, gave fresh emphasis to this commandment, when he said, "Thou shalt worship the Lord thy God, and him only shalt thou serve" (Matt. 4:10).

When we understand the purpose of God, we see that we are not dealing with a legal commandment. But, a principal whereby man discovers, by faith God does exist. God is indeed a reality. He is revealed to the searching heart that comes to him on the basis of faith.

Hebrews 11:16: "But without faith it is impossible to please him: for he that cometh to God must believe that he is, and that he is a rewarder of them that diligently seek him."

God's love is revealed in the person of his Son Christ Jesus when the searcher becomes a believer and a worshipper walking in the light of this revelation. Seeing that God is not some far-off mystical being, but is a loving, caring, heavenly Father, who is to always have first place in our lives.

We cannot treat God like a toy or give him attention only we feel like it. He demands first lace in our lives. Modern man zestfully explores outer space, the depths of the ocean, who seem quite content to live in a spiritual kindergarten, and play in a moral wilderness.

The scripture reminds us that the first commandment is not to be rejected or ignored. Romans 1:5: Warns not to worship the creature, but to worship the creator.

1 John 5:21:__ The apostle john writes, "Keep yourselves from idols."

2. *Thou Shalt Not Make Unto Thee Any Graven Image*

When God gave this commandment, he knew that the people had come out of a land of idol worship, and that they were going to a land where idols were common. Therefore, he commanded his people to abstain from graven gods.

While the first commandment deal with the object of worship. The third and forth with the method. The second centers on the manner of worship. It suggest that we are to worship God the person, not a symbolic graven image. We are to worship him in all his fullness through Jesus Christ.

Just as worship of the golden calf displeased God centuries ago. Worship of images of metal, wood, stone, displease him to-day. The crucifix or any other symbol of the Lord is totally inadequate. They do not show God in his fullness. We are to worship God in his majesty, worship in Spirit and truth.

3. *Thy Shalt Not Take the Name of the Lord Thy God in Vain*

Many think the only way to take the Lords name in vain, is to use profane language. But there are other ways of taking his name in vain. When making a profession of his name and not living up to it, that is vain. By failing to depart from sin and iniquity, that is vain. Matthew 15:7-9: "Ye hypocrite, well did Esaias prophecy of you, saying, This people draweth nigh unto me with their mouth, and honoureth me with their lips; but their heart is far from me. But in vain they do worship me . . ." *Talk the talk, but don't walk the walk!*

Scripture declares that the Lord will not hold one guiltless that take his name in vain. Hebrew 10:31: "It is a fearful thing to fall into the hands of the living God."

4. *Remember the Sabbath Day, and Keep It Holy*

This commandment consists of two simple injunctions. Remember the Sabbath day . . . six days shall thy labor . . . From the beginning, it has been the will of God for man to labor. Adam was to dress and keep the garden of Eden. Also, it has been his original intent that man should regularly cease from work to rest and worship. One can only mature to their fullest stature and fulfill the ideal relationship with God, only, as we work and worship.

Under the Law, man was to stop work and keep the Sabbath, which was the last day of the week. Under grace, the church age, this is the only commandment that changed when Jesus was crucified and rose on the first day of the week. It became the Lord's day. In the church age, Sunday is the Sabbath, and man is to live holy every day. Jesus said, "The Sabbath was made for man, and not man for the Sabbath."

5. *Honor Thy Father and Thy Mother*

The fact that children should honor their parents is basely universal. Most societies do recognize the importance of obedient children.

The first four commandments have reference to God. The last five to our neighbor. In between stands the fifth. It is liked to the first four, because of the young child. It is from the parent that a young child must learn to trust and obey God. The child must obey the parent. Ephesians 6:1: "Children, obey you parents in the Lord, for this is right."

Then verse 2: "Honor thy father and thy mother." The importance of the word *obedience* is almost more than the mind can grasp. God created man with the wonderful liberty of will, that he might obey him. Obedience to God will lead to enjoyment to him. It is the parents' responsibility to cultivate and develop his honor, respect, and obedience in the child. Because he/she cannot yet honor him.

Nor can he/she honor all persons. He/she can only honor what they see to be worthy of honor. This is the parents high calling, *Always* to live . . . speak . . . and act . . . that honor may be given spontaneously and unconsciously. This can only be when in a quite humble spirit the parent lives as in God's presence. Walking worthy of their calling.

6. *Thou Shalt Not Kill*

The precious gift of human life, which God brought into existence, when he created Adam and Eve became the object of his divine protection in his sixth commandment. Through his Law, he threw walls of protection around life. Murder was no precept known to Adam and Eve while they were still in the state of righteousness, they were created perfect—both in body and spirit. There was an inward urge to honor the divine gift of life. But the urge was crushed by sin, and as a result, that the human heart began to operate in the opposite direction.

The sixth commandment condemns the accomplished act of murder; whether it proceeds from open violence or premeditation.

Exodus 21:12-15:

12. He that smiteth a man, so that he die, shall be surely put to death.
13. And if a man lie not in wait, but God deliver him unto his hand, then I will appoint thee a place wither he shall flee.
14. But if a man come presumptuously upon a neighbor, to slay him with guile; thou shat take him from mine altar, that he may die.
15. And he that smiteth his father, or his mother, shall be surely put to death.

Looking into the Scripture in the New Testament, thou shalt not kill, goes beyond the mere act of taking the life of another. It forbids hatred, wither based on an offense or not. It extends to forbid abuse language, which kills influence and honor.

Jesus warned not to address one's brother as a fool or to say to him raca, a term of contempt used by the Jews.

Matthew 5:21-22, *Words of Jesus:* "Ye have heard that it was said of them of old time, Thou shall not kill; and whosoever shall kill shall be in danger of the judgment."

But I say unto you, That whosoever is angry with his brother without cause shall be in danger of the judgment: and whosoever shall say unto his brother, raca, shall be in danger of hell fire.

1 John 3:15, "Whosoever hateth his brother is a murderer: and ye know that no murderer hath eternal life abiding in him."

Life is precious and is protected by God. It is placed at the head of the human relations commandment, not as being the highest earthly possession, but as being the bases of existence.

In this life, the personality is subject to being attached. Therefore, with unquestioned clarity, God's command still goes out, "Thou shalt not kill."

7. *Thou Shalt Not Commit Adultery*

The Ten Commandments were given after the Israelites had been liberated from political oppression and from spiritual bondage. To preserve their redemption, it was necessary for them to live according to God's law. Among these, the seventh, an attempt to preserve the sanctity of marriage by condemning adultery, which has been defined as sexual unfaithfulness of a married person.

The sexual laxity of our time has eroded the cutting edge of moral and spiritual values. The home which heretofore was seen as the symbol of stability has been assailed, ridiculed, and dismembered.

But in the midst of what have become today's socially accepted sinful practices, nudity, companion swapping, mixed group orgies, and open homosexuality, a flood of liberal laws advocating abortion, there still stands an unchanging holy proclamation, *"Thou shalt not commit adultery."*

Adultery does not come by chance; It comes as a byproduct of gradual dissatisfaction between two people. In the unbeliever, adultery is pathetic. In the Christian, it is tragic. If there is no internal spirit defense, passion which lurks in the depth of the human sinful nature will jump out, tearing the soul apart. Those who disregard the law of God, trying to find ways to rationalize their wickedness. Leave them with horrible sense of guilt and loss.

A successful marriage requires a great amount of common sense, compassion, and, above all, faith in God. With an inner desire to abide by "the Word of God," the scripture offers some important guidelines:

Hebrews 13:4: "Marriage is honorable in all, and the bed undefiled: but whoremongers and adulterers God will judge."

1 Corinthians 7:3: "Let the husband render unto his wife due benevolence and likewise also the wife unto her husband."

Ephesians 5:22: "Wives, submit yourselves unto your own husbands, as unto the Lord."

Then verse 25: "Husbands, love your wives, even as Christ also loved the church, and gave himself for it."

Men and women alike can keep themselves pure, if they allow God to be in control of their lives.

8. *Thou Shalt Not Steal*

Here are four simple words of command. There is no need for a lengthy interpretation of it. It is very simple, yet profound, for it reveals God's concern for each person's right to own and posses goods, without the fear that they may be taken from them. This command prohibits secret or open removal of things of another; also, prohibits injury to them.

Paul declares that one should "plow in hope." That is, one should expect a return for their labor (1 Cor. 9:10).

So, in order to protect this right of everyone to pursue their occupation with hope and lawful gain, God has given laws to regulate our conduct toward the rights of others.

In Exodus, chapter twenty-two, God's laws judge the thief, demanded punishment for the thief, and provided restitution for the victim.

Paul's exhortation is found in Ephesians 4:28: "Let him that stole steal no more: but rather let him labour, working with his hands the thing which is good, that he may have to give to him that needeth."

9. *Thou Shalt Not Bear False Witness Against Neighbor*

This commandment is very forceful, personal, and simple to the extent that no one can mistake its intention. It says explicitly, "*Thy shall not bear false witness,*" and the last phase is just as plain as the first, "*against thy neighbor.*"

This is quite a message. It should be remembered that it is a god-given warning to all who seek to destroy a person by falsifying their character or to lie in any form for personal advantage or gain. God placed his disapproval on lying in the Garden of Eden, and until this day has not changed his attitude toward lying. Lying is wicked, and in all cases, sinful.

Revelation 21:8: "... all liars shall have their part in the lake which burneth with fire and brimstone ..."

The commandment not to lie is contained in both the New and Old Testaments. God has always hated lying, and what a folly of classifying lies; some call them big or little, black or white, still some call the harmless or harmful kind. The day one starts to categorizing lies is the day one is in trouble. The commandment is, "*Thou Shalt Not Bear False Witness,*" plain and simple.

Lies that are buried in the silent chambers of the past will rise again, rise to condemn the false tongue. Jesus said that there is nothing hidden that shall not be made known.

Good Christians do not go around talebearing and helping out the false witness. Lying is of the Devil. Liars do the work of the Devil. Jesus said, "I am the truth" (John 14:6).

Truth is the spiritual equipment of a fully armed child of God. One lie, most times, needs the support of another, where truth never changes and stands over against and opposing the lie. Truth is God. Lying is of the Devil.

Paul says in Ephesians 4:25: "put away lying and speak every man the truth with his neighbor."

10. *Thou Shalt Not Covet*

Covetousness is the inordinate desire for that which belongs to another so that one would, if possible, take it from them and make it theirs. Further, it is the over strong desire for more, which desire is uncontrolled by reason or the Word of God.

Covetousness makes one seek to *nest high* in order to fulfill prideful ambition. It is the chief ingredient to greed, which is a transgression of God's law.

Covetousness is dynamic. It can be observed in its progressive root meaning. It begins simply with the delight in beauty, which soon turns to wish, which itself involves into fervency of mind, progressing into the setting of the heart and then lust. Neither does it stop there; lust is then acted out in fraud. Then, whatever it takes to obtain it is selfish desire.

Covetousness in the scripture is in the same category with adultery, fornication, uncleanness, lasciviousness, idolatry, witchcraft, hatred, variance, emulations, wrath, strife, seditions, heresies, envying, murder, drunkenness; they which do such things shall not inherit the kingdom of God (Gal. 5:19-21).

Each of the *Ten Commandments* deal with man's relationship to God and man. They are God's moral law, defining man's duty to God and man; they are timeless and unchanging for all time with exception of the Sabbath.

Chapter Eight

The Tabernacle in the Wilderness

Introduction

The Israelites remained at Sinai more than a year. During this time, they were occupied chiefly in learning the many details of the law which they were to follow ever after. In this interval, one of the most important developments was the building of the Tabernacle, the chief purpose of which was to represent God as dwelling in the midst of his people, and is a great type and shadow of Jesus Christ, who was to come.

The Tabernacle itself stood in the center of rectangular space enclosed by a substantial wall. The Israelites camped round about it. The Tabernacle will represent the way God ordained that man should approach him.

Plan of Israel's Camp
{numbers chapters 2 and 3}

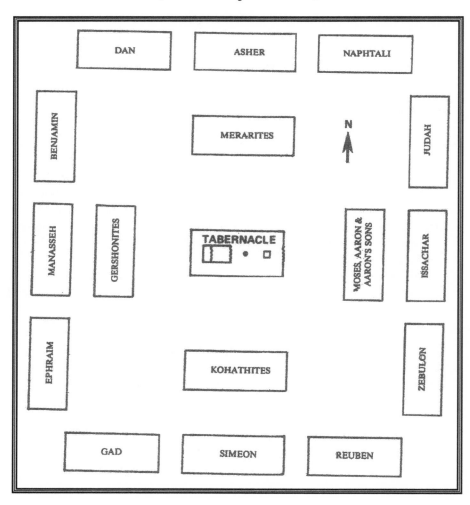

The Tabernacle in the Wilderness

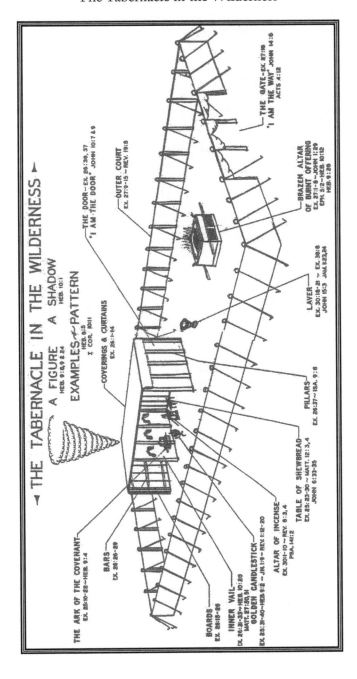

◄ THE TABERNACLE IN THE WILDERNESS ►

A FIGURE A SHADOW
HEB. 9:8 & 24 HEB. 10:1

EXAMPLES ◄ PATTERN
HEB. 6:5
I COR. 10:11

COVERINGS & CURTAINS
EX. 25:1-14

THE DOOR ─ EX. 26:36, 37
"I AM THE DOOR" JOHN 10:7 & 9

OUTER COURT
EX. 27:9-15 ~ REV. 19:8

THE GATE ─ EX. 27:16
"I AM THE WAY" JOHN 14:6
ACTS 4:12

BRAZEN ALTAR
OF BURNT OFFERING
EX. 27:1-8 ~ JOHN 1:29
EPH. 5:2 ~ HEB. 10:12
HEB. 9:26

LAVER
EX. 30:18-21 ~ EX. 38:8
JOHN 15:3 JAM. 1:23,24

PILLARS
EX. 26:37 ~ ISA. 9:6

TABLE OF SHEWBREAD
EX. 25: 23-30 ~ MATT. 12: 3,4
JOHN 6:33-35

ALTAR OF INCENSE
EX. 30:1-10 ~ REV. 8:3, 4
PSA. 141:2

GOLDEN CANDLESTICK
EX. 25: 31-40 ~ HEB. 9:2 ~ JN. 1:9 ~ REV. 1:12-20

INNER VAIL
DL. 26: 31-33 ~ HEB. 10:20
MATT. 27:50,51

BOARDS
EX. 26:15-20

BARS
EX. 26: 26-29

THE ARK OF THE COVENANT
EX. 25:10-22 ~ HEB. 9:4

The "*Tabernacle form of Worship*" are figures of that which was to come. (Heb. 9:8-9).

Heb. 10:1: It was a shadow or principle of God's future plans_ . . .

The "*Tabernacle*" and the "*Tabernacle form of Worship*" were examples and patterns established by God for the benefit of those in the ages to come (1 Cor. 10:11, Heb. 8:5).

The arrangement of the Tabernacle furniture falls into a perfect cross.

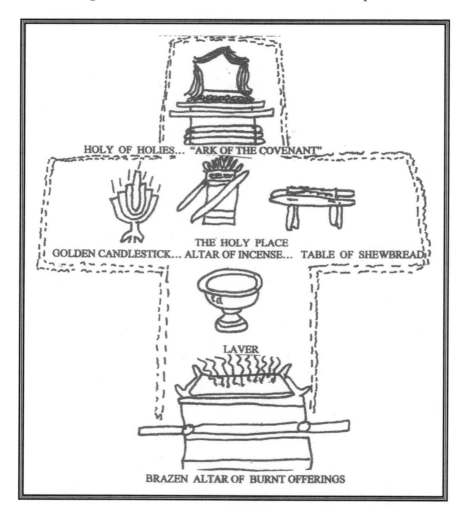

Hebrews 8:5: ". . . Moses was admonished of God when he was about to make the Tabernacle: For, See, said he, that thou make all things according to the pattern showed to thee in the mount."

When God spends much time on any subject, we may be sure it is of tremendous importance. Over one-third of the book of Exodus is devoted to the details of the Tabernacle.

Building the Tabernacle

There must have been excitement in the camp. Imagine a camp of over one million people talking about building a tabernacle. It was to be the very center of the camp. This was to be where God was to meet with the people.

A question to ask ourselves, "Is God the center of our life?"

The principle act in the *Tabernacle Worship* was the slaying of the sacrificial lamb. It was not until Jesus, the Savior came that the full meaning of the Tabernacle could be understood. When men broke the law, God revealed his plan whereby they once again could worship him. Today, Jesus is the only meeting place between a *Holy God* and a lost sinner. St. John 14:6, Jesus said, "I am the way, the truth, and the life: no man cometh to the Father but by me."

Now let us imagine ourselves entering the court through the gate. We must begin with the way in. The gate was the only entrance.

It was 150 x 75 x 7½ feet high. The outer court fabric was a fine linen material. According to Revelation 19, fine linen represents the righteousness of the Bride of Christ. We know from 2 Corinthians 5:21, our righteousness is none other than Jesus Christ, "For he hath made him to be sin for us, who knew no sin, that we might be made the righteousness of God in him." Therefore, the linen of the court represents the purity and the absolute righteousness of Jesus Christ separating us from the world. The linen was made of flax. Flax is grown from the earth. Here is a picture of the earthly ministry of Jesus. The outer court kept all that was defiled away from God's place of worship. The first act of worship was through the court gate to the place of the blood sacrifice, the Brazen Altar. Today, no member of the human race can worship God except through the provision God himself has made, That being, the sacrifice of his son on the cross; it is through Christ Jesus that we reach God the Father. There is no other way. The outer court also spoke protection in as much as it enclosed those who came to God with their offering.

The pillars which were caped with silver held the linen in place; the linen representing believers in Jesus Christ, holding up for the world to see the righteousness of God which is Jesus Christ. The world must see Jesus in us.

Let Us Now Take a Close at the Picture

What do we find relative to these pillars that led us to believe that they represent believers?

First: Silver in the scripture speaks of redemption. We should remember that all the materials for the Tabernacle was given as a freewill offering; all except for the silver. The same amount of silver was required of each Israelite for the building of the Tabernacle. During those days, slaves were bought with silver. Joseph's brothers sold him for silver. You and I were purchased out of the slave market of sin with the redemption blood of Jesus, who Judas sold for thirty pieces of silver. Jesus paid it all, all to him we owe.

The pillars were made of brass. The scripture is not clear as to whether these were solid brass or shittim wood overlaid with brass. In any event, we will see later how shittim wood is a picture of humanity. This being true, these pillars again speak of believers here on earth.

Remember the brazen serpent held upon a pole in the wilderness; how all that looked upon it would live? This was a picture of Jesus bearing our judgment on the cross. St John 3:14, "As Moses lifted up the serpent in the wilderness, even so must the Son of man be lifted up."

These pillars were set in brass, speaking of judgment underneath. Once we repent of our sins, they are under the blood of Jesus; forgiven never to be remembered.

By Way of Summary

We now have a picture of the believer who has been crowned with redemption; although condemned to die, now have judgment of God under foot. Therefore, being justified by faith, we have peace with God through our Lord Jesus Christ. Now, as believers, we are holding up to a dying world *the Righteousness of God*.

The Court Gate

Exodus 27:16: "And for the court shall be hanging twenty cubits, of blue, purple, and scarlet and fine twined linen, wrought with needlework: and their pillars shall be four, and Their sockets four."

The court gate is the only way in. It was thirty feet wide and seven and one-half feet high. Jesus said: "I am the way" He is our only way into a right relationship with God the Father. He was thirty years old when he began his ministry here on earth. The wide gate is a picture of the easy and simple way of salvation offered to all mankind.

Now, with all this in mind let us take a look at the colors of the gate: fine white linen embroidered in blue, purple, and scarlet. Why these colors? Certainly, God did not choose them by random. The fine white linen speaks of Jesus righteousness. The blue, purple, and scarlet certainly speak of him also. This is especially true when we realize that theses colors are found no where else in the outer court.

In harmony with what we are about to say, first let us be reminded of the four gospels: Matthew, Mark, Luke, and John.

Matthew: Portrays Jesus as *King of the Jews*.

Is sometimes called, *The Kingdom Gospel*.

Mark: Pictures Jesus as the servant, obedient to death.

Luke: Pictures him as, *The Son of Man*.

John: Depicts or portrays him as, *The Son of God*.

Now, with these facts relative to the gospels established, let us take a careful look at the colors woven into the fine white linen gate curtains.

The Blue—represents Jesus as the heavenly one found in the Gospel of John; *The Son of God*.

The Purple—which was, and is even today, the color of royalty, so, representing in type Jesus as, *The Son of David* as we find him in the gospel of Matthew.

The Scarlet—color of blood or sacrifice. Certainly pictures for us Jesus as we find him in the gospel of Mark, the servant obedient even unto death.

White—which represents purity and righteousness, which we find in Luke's gospel, *The Holy One* and *The Sinless One*.

These colors as we find them here in the gate curtains represent the Lord Jesus Christ in this four-fold sense. No guards were needed at the gate, for it is to whosoever will come. God has placed no barriers to anyone who will come.

The four pillars of the gate, which support the curtains, represent the four writers of the gospels. The scripture does not indicate that the pillars of the gate were any different from any of the other pillars. Certainly, the writers of the gospels were sinners saved by the grace of God, just as every one else.

The Gate—The Way

Again, let us remember the words of Jesus: "I am the way, the truth, and the life, no man cometh to the Father but by me." *He is the Son of God—the Holy One.*

He is the one who shed his blood for whosoever will come to him. *He is the Lamb of God!*

The Brazen Altar and The Laver

I. The Brazen Altar of Burnt Offering, Exodus 27:1-8

    a. Size: 7½ x 7½ feet
             4½ feet high;
    b. Material: Shittim wood, brass, and horns;
    c. The lamb and fire

II. The Laver, Exodus 30:17-21

    a. Material: Brass [size not given].
    b. The Water: [type of God's Word].

Supplement to the Outline

When we think of an altar, we immediately think of worship. An altar is a place of humiliation, a place of submission to something or someone. This is what happens when we come to Jesus Christ for salvation. We realize that we are sinners and accept *God's Sacrificial Lamb the Lord and Savior Jesus Christ* for our salvation.

Immediately after the priest offered the sacrifice on the *Brazen Altar*, his next appointment was at the *Laver*. We shall see how the laver is a symbol of God's Word.

As we come to the outer court, we see the Brazen Altar. The shittim wood from which this altar is constructed gives a beautiful picture of Jesus Christ's Humanity. Shittim wood being an indestructible type of wood will withstand heat. Our Lord's body withstood the divine fire of God's judgment—A judgment which should have been ours. Because he did it, "There is therefore now no condemnation to them to whom which are in Christ Jesus" (Rom. 8:4).

Shittim wood was a desert shrub. This shrub possessed a long tap root reaching deep down to the subterranean dampness. How well this reminds us of the prophet Isaiah, when he wrote prophetically concerning Jesus's humanity, ". . . as a root out of dry ground: he had no form nor comeliness (Isa. 53:2).

As we come through the gate to the outer court, we see the Brazen Altar. Here, the one who had sinned brought the animal, one without blemish. This animal was to die in his place.

The law said in Exodus 18:4: "The soul that sinneth it shall die." So the sinner comes confessing his/her sin and has brought an animal offering as their substitute. The Brazen Altar was the place where the sacrificial lamb was slain.

Here, we have a picture of Jesus on the cross, where he bore the plenty for whosoever will come. The iniquity of all was laid upon him.

Just as the Brazen Altar was the only place where the children of Israel could receive postponement of divine judgment for their sin, so is the cross of Jesus—the Lamb of God—is the only place where man can come today to receive forgiveness for sin.

When one realizes he/she is a sinner, they come to Jesus as the *Sacrificial Lamb* for salvation, repents of the sin in their life; all is forgiven and forgotten. Romans 8:1, "There is therefore now no condemnation to them which are in Christ Jesus."

The Horns

These were placed at each corner of the top of the *Brazen Altar*. Why were they there? What was their purpose? It is not clear of their function. But it is quite clear of their meaning. These horns were found only on this *Brazen Altar* and the *Altar of Incense*. In the seventh chapter of Daniel's writings, he spoke of power of kings' horns. Later, we shall find the *Altar of Incense* representing prayer.

The act of prayer is indeed one of the highest privileges of one's Christian life. Often, we sing, "Take it to the Lord in prayer." But, do we? God has opened up a way into his presence for all who care to avail themselves to such access. He said, "ask and it shall be given you, seek and ye shall find, knock and it shall be opened unto you" (Matt. 7:7).

Then in verse 8: "For everyone that asketh receiveth; and he that seeketh findeth; and to him that knocketh it shall be opened."

Why not take advantage of such a great privilege?

Jesus never taught his disciples to preach, but he did teach them how to pray.

One does not have to wait on some man or office to pray. Man can go to God through Christ Jesus at anytime, anywhere.

Prayer must be presented in the name of Jesus and must ascend out of a pure heart. Prayer and purity are partners. It is not what we try to be when we are praying. But what we are before we go to the Lord in prayer. Then, too, prayer must be more than our own will or wishes. It must be pleasing to God, must be according to his word. That is why we need to know what the scripture says. There are times when we do not know what to pray; that is when the Holy Spirit can make intercession for us.

Prayer avails for our need—need of our body, covers the need of our home, enables us to face responsibilities, and will remove those mountains that come in our life. Prayer is simply talking with God. Find you a place where you can talk with God. Go there often and expect him to meet you there.

So let us pray for all necessary courage, hope, and faith. Get hold of the horns of the altar of God. Do not give up. Hold on!

We know the power of the blood of Jesus, of which the *Altar of Burnt Offerings* is symbolic.

Ephesians 5:2: "Christ hath given himself for us an offering and sacrifice to God."

Through him, we receive power—power over sin

Hebrews 9:28: "So Christ was once offered to bear the sins of many."

John 1:29: "Behold, the Lamb of God, which taketh away the sin of the world.'

So when we need power, power to overcome whatever, take hold of the horns of the altar of God as it were. Hold on. Discover the power of prayer.

The Laver

Exodus 30:17-18: "And the Lord spake unto Moses, saying, Thou shalt also make a laver of brass, foot also of bras, to wash withal: and thou shalt put it between the tabernacle of the congregation and the altar, and thou shalt put water therein."

The question now confronting us is, "How does this laver speak to us representing God's Word, in so much as it is brass?"

To begin with, we are judged as sinners, condemned at every turn, eternally lost. This is why God requires an infinite sacrifice to justify that one may be justified in his eyes. That sacrifice is Jesus Christ, who gave his life on the cross at Calvary.

Before the priest could enter the Holy Place, he must wash his hands at the laver. As he washes his hands, he could see himself in the water.

Just as the priest could see himself as he washes his hands, the Word of God, the Bible, will show each of us just where we are with God. That is why we should study the scripture, that we may know just what God requires of each of us, that we may know what his promises are, and that we may know what the requirements are that we may receive them.

James 1:22-25: "But be ye doers of the word, and not hearer only, deceiving your own selves. For if any be a hearer of the word, and not a doer, he is like unto a man beholding his natural face in a glass. For he beholdeth himself, and goeth his way, and straightway forgetteth what manner of man he was. But whoso looketh into the perfect law of liberty, and continueth therein, he being not a forgetful hearer, but a doer of the work, this man shall be blessed in his deed."

It was mandatory for the priest to wash his hands at the laver before entering the Holy Place. If he failed to wash his hands and entered into the Holy Place, he would die (Exod. 30:20-21).

In the New Testament, believers are called priest (Rev. 1:5-8).

Should the believer fail to come to God's Word regularly, then they will die spiritually. Jesus said in John 15:3: "Now ye are cleansed through the word which I have spoken unto you."

Ephesians 5:26: "That he might sanctify and cleanse it with the washing of the word."

Certainly, we need to approach God's Word in an atmosphere of holy reverence, trusting him to show us ourselves.

Let us now look at the picture before us. We have the priest washing his hands at the laver. Seeing himself as he is. Cleansing himself of any defilement. That he may enter the Holy Place.

The Laver—A Figure—A Shadow

Hebrews 9:8-9: "The Holy Ghost this signifying, that the way into the holiest of all was not yet made manifest, while as the first tabernacle was yet standing. Which was a figure for the time then present, in which were offered both gifts and sacrifices, which could not make him that did service perfect as pertaining to the conscience."

Then Hebrews 10:1: "For the law having a shadow of good things to come."

With these scriptures in mind, let us now look again at the laver. Repeating from a previous lesson, no where is the size of weight of the laver is given. We just know that it was made of brass and filled with water, and that it represents the Word of God.

It is important that we remember that the priest was not qualified to enter the Holy Place until he washed his hands at the laver. You see, a stop at the Brazen Altar was not enough. After the sacrifice was made, then he must stop at the Laver.

1 John 1:5: "If we confess our sins, he is faithful and just to forgive us our sins and cleanse us from all unrighteousness." That is the first step. *The New Birth* forgiven of the sins which we committed. But there is still that inbred sin from Adam.

In salvation, *The New Birth* one is taken out of sin; pardon takes place, justification takes place through Jesus, regeneration takes place. We are now alive and adopted into the family of God.

Ephesians 2:19, "Now therefore ye are no more strangers and foreigners but fellow citizens with the saints and household of God."

See, in the *New Birth,* one is forgiven of all sins committed and placed into the family of God. One's old record is wiped out. God will never remember them any more. But, there is still that inbred sin from Adam. The Believer, though forgiven and is a new creature in Christ Jesus, may still struggle with habits learned over a lifetime. These habits which have become standard daily practices can be difficult to change. So, what is one to do?

Sanctification is the Way Out

Let us pause here and take a look at the experience of sanctification.

To sanctify is to make clean—to be made holy—to set apart for a holy use.

This cannot be accomplished apart from the blood of Jesus Christ and working of the Holy Ghost working in one's life.

The experience and doctrine of sanctification was planned by God the Father, provided by God the Son, and is applied by God the Holy Ghost.

For the soul, it is a cleansing from the inbred sin from Adam. This is done through the blood of Jesus Christ. It is a definite second work of grace for the soul.

For the spirit and the body, it is a progressive work. It is a separation from all evil to a life of holiness. This one does themselves. As one learns the Word of God and applies it to their life, the body and spirit is sanctified. We are instructed in the scripture to walk in the light as we see the light. So, as said, for the body and spirit, it is a progressive work. The Apostle Paul said, "I sanctify myself daily."

1 Thessalonians 5:23: "And the very God of peace sanctify you wholly: and I pray God your whole spirit and soul and body be preserved blameless unto the coming of our Lord Jesus Christ."

The whole person—*spirit, soul, body.*

The *soul* is the part of man called, "*the seat of life, the intellect,* and *the emotion and will.*"

The *spirit* is that part of man that "*thinks, desires,* and *understands.*"

In accepting God, one must become God conscious, then be spiritual receptive and spiritually responsive.

The *body* is the visible part of man. The *soul* manifests its desire through the *body* as the *spirit* permits.

The experience of Sanctification is not for the sinner. It is for the believer—one that has been born again. St. John 17:15: Jesus praying for the disciples said: "I pray not for the world, but for them which thou hast given me, for thy are thine."

Verse 16: "They are not of the world."

Verse 17: "Sanctify them through thy word, thy word is truth."

Not only did Jesus pray for the disciples to be sanctified for. In verse 20, he says: "Neither pray I for these alone, but for them also which shall believe on me through their word." As the Christian hears the word and acts upon it by faith and obedience, they are sanctified in spirit and body.

2 Corinthians 7:1: "dearly beloved, let us cleanse ourselves from all filthiness and of the flesh and spirit." *Remember I ask you to hold the thought of the priest at the laver?*

God did not wash his hands; the priest washed his hands; God removes the inbred sin from our soul . . . He gave us his word that we might see ourselves and cleanse ourselves.

The people at Corinth were instructed to cleanse themselves of the spirit and of the flesh . . . they were sanctified in soul . . .

Chapters six and nine, we are told that they had also received the Holy Ghost. Now they are to take care of the spirit and body.

How?

We are given instruction in the scripture to walk in the light as we see the light.

The body has no capacity for knowledge of right or wrong . . . It has no power to accept or reject . . . It is a servant of the spirit.

Scripture instructs us: "*That everyone should know how to posses their vessel in sanctification and honor.*"

This is a personal message . . ."*Know how to posses your vessel.*"

How do we that? Through the Word of God . . . *When you are sanctified, it will not change the world, but you will see the world through different eyes.*

Ezekiel 36:26-27: "A new heart also will I give you and a new spirit I will put within you: and I will take away the stony heart out of your flesh, and will give you a heart of flesh and will put my Spirit within you, and cause you to walk in my statues, and ye shall keep my judgment, and do them" As the priest washed his hand seeing himself in the laver, before entering the holy place, let us daily take God's Word—"the Bible"—apply it to ourselves, walking in the light of it. Serving him in this body that he has given us, knowing in the next life we shall have a new body fashioned in the likeness of his.

The Tabernacle Structure

Exodus 26:

    I.   The Boards and Bars:

        1.   Material: Gold and wood, sockets of silver;

   II. The Curtains:

        1.   Inner or first curtain: Fine-twined linen;
        2.   The second curtain: Goat's hair;

  III. The Covering:

        1.   Ram's skin dyed red, hidden from view;
        2.   Badger's skins, outer covering (unattractive)

  IV. The Door:

        1.   The linen;
        2.   The pillars;

Supplement to the Outline

The Tabernacle was constructed according to a divine plan wherein Jehovah God was the supreme architect and Moses was the general contractor. Moses was given many skilled workers, among whom was Bezaleel, his foreman. This man was especially endowed with the Holy Spirit. Similarly, we are workers with Jesus Christ in building his church. Christian service is not so much working for the Lord as working with him.

This structure was forty-five feet long, fifteen feet wide, and fifteen feet high, The holy place was thirty feet long and the holy of holies fifteen feet long. The holy of holies constituted that area behind the Vail wherein was the *Ark of the Covenant.*

The Boards and Bars

The boards which were assembled vertically and locked together, constructed the structural members of the Tabernacle. These were fabricated from shittim (acacia) wood overlaid with pure gold. The boards were seated into silver sockets.

Within the *holy place* of worship, we shall find the total absence of brass. There is no place for divine judgment here. Judgment was taken care of at the *Brazen Altar.*

The priest who had washed his hands at the laver is now qualified to worship God in the Tabernacle. These priests represent the believers of today. Revelation 1:6 and 5:10 let us to know that believers of today are priest. As such, we can come boldly to the Throne of God, through Jesus Christ.

The high priest, beginning with Aaron, is in every way a type of Jesus Christ, our high priest, who ever liveth to make intersession for us.

Material: Gold and Wood—Sockets of Gold

When we look at the wood boards covered in gold, we immediately think of the Lord Jesus Christ, who was both human and divine.

Let us see in these boards, a picture of the believer as well. These many boards that are interlocked are seated in silver sockets. When one repents of their sins, accepts Jesus into their life, *born again*, then they become children of God. As such, we are bound together with Jesus redemptive work. In being bound together, our love for one another is the direct product of bonds of Calvary. As the boards of silver, we are resting in Jesus redemptive power that he has provided for us.

These boards, which are overlaid with gold, speak to us of our humanity clothed in divinity. Of course, our divinity is now veiled. But, when we see him face-to-face, then we shall be like him, for we shall see him as he is.

The Bars, Gold and Wood

Here again, we have the wood overlaid with gold. We are told there are five bars on each side of the Tabernacle. These bars are attached to the boards. (The figure five is frequently representative of the grace of God.) Here we see a picture of the Lord binding all of his children together.

The inner curtain which was visible from inside the Tabernacle was made of fine white linen. Colors of blue, purple, and red were interwoven.

As an integral part of the curtain, we find Cherubim. What does this mean? Well, Jehovah the great designer is showing to us in type a picture of the Lord. We see, again, his divine righteousness in the fine white linen. This Egyptian linen of which has been said the world cannot produce today. Also, we have the colors of blue, purple, and red representing Jesus. These colors are the same as in the outer court gate. Only the outer court gate had no Cherubim. Why do we find them here in these curtains?

Cherubim speak of the guards of his holiness or his holiness vindicated. The truth is not difficult to establish when we remember God place Cherubim at the east gate of the garden of Eden when he drove Adam and Eve out of the garden.

Also, Cherubim were placed as guards of the throne of God when Lucifer lost his position in heaven.

The inner court curtain was held together with fasteners of gold. The scripture is careful to tell us that the Tabernacle is one Tabernacle that is one perfect whole (Exod. 26:6).

First, here is a picture of Christ and his bride, the church; In a greater sense, as him head of the church. The fasteners of gold speak of his divinity, our worship. As was the priest who worship in the Tabernacle, we must enter in Christ.

Second, the second curtain was made of goat hair, which is completely hidden from view of the priest inside the Tabernacle. The goat hair depicts the blackness of sin. The Palestinian goat was black and still is today. In scripture, the goat is used in a bad sense.

Exodus 26:12-13: We read that the goat hair curtain was made to hang down over the edge of the Tabernacle a distance of one cubit. This portion was exposed to the view of all Israelite encampment.

Here again, we see, Jesus Christ one who knew no sin—yet became sin for all mankind—one who lived here on earth for a short period, exposed to man's insults and finally death on the cross. To the outside world, he was despised and rejected.

The Coverings were durable materials than the curtains. They provided adequate protection for the Tabernacle. Ram's skin dyed red rest upon the goat hair. The outer covering was *badger skin;* the color is not revealed, but it must have been unattractive to the observer on the outside. The badger skin provided adequate protection from all of the world's elements, just as true Jesus Christ shields his own from all the onslaughts of the devil.

The Door is the way acceptable worship of God; the way of communion and fellowship with him, for the purpose of man's creation.

Jesus said, "I am the door." and we know that he is the way to life eternal. Not only is he an entrance to a happy life while here on earth, but to eternal life beyond this life.

The Pillars: There were five for the door; they were covered with gold, speaking of divinity; were set in brass, speaking of Jesus's victory over our judgment, which was placed on him; judgment is now under his feet.

In connection with the five pillars, Isaiah 9:6: *Five names are given to the Lord*:

> *Wonderful;*
>> *Counselor;*
>>> *The Mighty God;*
>>>> *The Mighty Father;*
>>>>> *The Prince of Peace;*

So it is clear to see the simple message of salvation in the Tabernacle!

The Golden Candlestick

Exodus 25:31-40, 27:20-21

    I.   Material: Beaten gold.

        1.   The shaft.
        2.   The branches.

    II. The seven lamps.

    III. The oil for the lamps.

        1.   Made of beaten olives.
        2.   The only light.

Supplement to the Outline

The Golden Candlestick was a very important item within the Holy Place of the Tabernacle. Like all other furniture it was very costly. At the end of the central shaft were lamps that contained oil. The branches and the shaft were beaten into series of knobs, bowls, and flowers. An equal number of these constituted each branch.

Let us now approach the interior of the *Holy Place*. There is no brass here. No place for divine judgment. In the *Holy Place*, there are three pieces of furniture:

> *The Golden Candlestick;*
> *The Altar of Incense;*
> *The Table of Shewbread;*

First, we will take a look at *the* Golden Candlestick. The weight was ninety talents: Ninety Hebrew talents represent approximately ninety-four pounds.

Here again, we have the gold representing the divinity of the Lord Jesus Christ. This was not just mere gold; it was beaten gold that had endured punishment.

Of the Lord Jesus Christ, we read in Isaiah 53:1-7:

1. Who hath believed our report? And to whom is the arm of the Lord revealed?
2. For he shall grow up before him as a tender plant, and as a root out of a dry ground: he hath no form nor comeliness: and when we shall see him, there is no beauty that we should desire him.
3. He is despised and rejected of men, a man of sorrows, and acquainted with grief; and we hid as it were our faces from him; he was despised, and we esteemed him not.
4. Surely he hath bore our grief, and carried our sorrow: yet we did esteem him stricken, smitten of God, and afflicted.
5. But he was wounded for our transgressions, he was bruised for our iniquities, the chastisement of our peace was upon him, and with his stripes we are healed.
6. All we like sheep have gone astray, we have turned everyone to his own way; and the Lord hath laid on him the iniquity of us all.
7. He was oppressed, and he was afflicted, yet he opened not his mouth: he is brought as a lamb before the slaughter, and as sheep before the shearers is dumb, so he opened not his mouth.

Then, in verse 10: "Yet it pleased the Lord to bruse him." *Why?* "When thou shalt make his soul an offering for sin."

God did all this to Jesus to bring the church into existence. It cost infinite suffering to bring about the birth of the church, who will be *The Bride of Jesus.*

The weight of the candlestick was ninety talents which represents approximately thirty thousand dollars in value, based on U.S. gold standards.

In view of all this, we are compelled to say, there are no limitations placed on the Lord Jesus Christ. He is omnipresent. Not only is he unlimited and unrestricted, his value is fathomless! The incarnate worth is immeasurable and is full of grace and truth. We are redeemed by his precious blood.

The Shaft of the Candlestick

This portion of the candlestick is the center stem from which the branches on each side is attached. John 15:5, Jesus said, "I am the vine ye are the branches."

In Revelation the first chapter, we read, "And in the midst of the seven candlesticks one like unto the Son of man" Then, in the gospel of Luke, Jesus is called the Son of man twenty-six times.

The Branches

There were seven of these. Its seven lights were not candles as one might think from their name. They were lamps burning beaten olive oil. This oil speaks of the Holy Spirit.

We are familiar with the parable of "*The Ten Virgins*" (Matt. 25:1-13).

The parable tells who could enter into the marriage, and who could not. The five foolish were unable to enter because they had no oil.

Then, too, Jesus says: "No man cometh to the Father except the Spirit draw him" It is the supernatural working of the Holy Spirit that must draw the individual. It was the Holy Spirit hovering over the water and the spoken Word of God that brought light to the world.

It was the same Holy Spirit that hovered over Mary, causing her to conceive and bring forth Jesus in the form of man; he who brought light into a sin-sick world.

We must remember that the Holy Spirit is a person. Ephesians 4:30, instructs us, "grieve not the Holy Spirit of God."

Matthew 5:14: "Ye are the light of the world." God needs individuals to shine forth his light in this dark and sinful world. Those who are living a life that others see Christ in them. As the moon reflects her light from the sun, we should reflect light of Jesus Christ. Matthew 5:13, Jesus said: "Ye are the salt of the earth," then admonished us in verse 16, "Let your light so shine before men, that they may see your good works, and glorify your heavenly Father which is in heaven." Back to the Holy Place, there are no windows, no natural light; the only light was that radiating from the candlestick. Then too, the priest could not have carried out his sacred duties of worship without light to see. The candlestick provided the light. I repeat, there is a total absence of natural light here in the Tabernacle. Only the supernatural light of the glorious gospel of Jesus Christ can illuminate our hearts and minds and prepare us for eternity. Education, culture, or wealth found in the natural world will never suffice. The Lord Jesus Christ as the light of the world in perfect cooperation with the Holy Spirit as chief executor will get the job done.

The seven lamps in Revelation 4:5: We read of the seven lamps of fire, which are the seven Spirits of God. Certainly, there is no spiritual light in the world today other than the Holy Spirit. He as it were, set on fire the children of God. Our efforts to witness effectively of him are useless only as the Holy Spirit motivates and directs.

Seven in the scripture is often symbolic of perfection or completeness. Where can we find any more significance attached to this number than in the seven lamps here in the Holy Place representing God, the Holy Spirit, dwelling in the church?

The Oil for the Lamp

The candlesticks would be useless without the oil for the lamp. We find the oil for the lamp mentioned in the book of Exodus, immediately after the outer court. Thus, illustrates for us, the Holy Spirit active in the life of the believer, after the believer has come for salvation by God's appointed way.

This oil was made from beaten olives, just as the candlestick was made from beaten gold. So, the oil being made from beaten olives, *could it be*, this represents the suffering of the Holy Spirit? We must always remember the Holy Spirit is the third person of the God Head with sense of feeling. Ephesians 4:30, "Grieve not the Holy Spirit." How it must have grieved the Holy Spirit as he watched the agony of Jesus on the cross.

As stated before, the only light in the Tabernacle was that of the candlestick, which gave the light for the priest to perform his sacred duties. Only the supernatural light of the glorious gospel of Jesus Christ can illuminate the human heart and mind.

The Altar of Incense

Exodus 30:1-10, Psalm 141:2, Revelation 8:3-4

    I.   Material and Size:

        1. Wood and Gold, 1½ x 1½ x 3 feet.
        2. The Horn.
        3. The Crown.

    II. Relative position.
    III. The Altar Fire.

Supplement to the Outline

We see from Psalm 2 and Revelation 8:3-4 how this Altar typifies prayer and worship. It is a small piece of furniture, but sufficiently large enough to serve the purpose. It is not the long prayers that avails much, but the prayer of faith. We are not heard for vain repetition, but the fervent prayer of a righteous man availeth much. The Golden Altar of Incense is a type of Christ in respect to the efficiency of his meditator work for us (Hebrews 7:25; 8:1).

The Altar of Incense

This was a small piece of furniture. 1½ x 1½ feet, 3 feet high, made of wood and overlaid with gold, but sufficiently large enough to serve its purpose.

On the altar was continual fire. Each morning and each evening when Aaron, the priest, went to care for the lamps of the Golden Candlesticks, he offered prayer for the people and burned sweet-smelling incense of the Golden Altar.

The Horns

The horns were at the four corners of the altar. They were similar to those on the Brazen Altar. These were also made of wood and overlaid with gold.

The horns of the Brazen Altar spoke of power in the blood, while the horns of the Golden Altar spoke of the power of prayer.

In 2 Samuel 22:3, we hear David singing about the horn of salvation. In the gospel of Luke, we read, "God has raised up a horn of salvation for us in the house of his servant David."

The gospel is the power of God unto salvation.

Once a year, on the Day of Atonement, these horns were sprinkled with blood from the Brazen Altar. God never forgets the suffering of his Son, Jesus Christ, endured for us. We must never forget the effect his blood which he shed for us.

It was Zacharias, father of John the baptizer, who made the prophecy in Luke 1:69: "And raised up an horn of salvation for us in the house of his servant David." Zacharias was a priest of God and would have been familiar with the Altar of Incense. Surely, it was the Holy Spirit that directed him to use the terminology, as he prophesied of Jesus Christ, "Raised up a horn of salvation for us."

The Crow

We are all acquainted with the generally accepted meaning of a crown, speaking of exaltation.

A golden crown was placed around the top of the Altar of Incense, which gives us a picture of Jesus Christ exalted. It is only because Jesus was resurrected and exalted to the right hand of God the Father that we can expect to realize the power of answered prayer.

Do you know that the Holy Spirit makes intercession for us? Listen to Romans 8:26: "Likewise the Spirit also helpeth our infirmities: for we know not what we should pray for as we ought: but the Spirit maketh intercession for us with groanings which cannot be uttered." We call it praying in the Spirit. The Holy Spirit speaks to Christ Jesus and Christ Jesus to the Father.

The Altar of Incense

This was placed according to divine plan. Just before the place of God's habitation, "The Holy of Holies." Our prayers are channeled directly to God the Father through Christ Jesus.

There is one vast difference between the altar in the Tabernacle and that in heaven. In the Tabernacle, we find a barrier—the veil that extended across the Tabernacle separating the Holy place from the Holy of Holies. At the crucifixion of Jesus, this veil was rent from top to bottom. As a result, we now have access to the Throne of God. We can approach the Throne of God anytime, anywhere. How different form the Holy of Holies in the Tabernacle. There, only the priest could enter, and only once a year could he enter the Holy of Holies, on the Day of Atonement, and only if he had applied the blood of the animal to atone for his sins.

The Altar Fire

The fire was taken from the Brazen Altar, from the outer court into the Holy Place. As the fire of the Altar of Incense was taken from the Brazen Altar, our prayers are effective today only because of the finished work of Jesus on the cross.

We are prone to think of Jesus as dying for our sins. This he did, for which we praise him. But, his death and his resurrection did much more for us. We now enjoy and submit our personal petitions to God the Father through Jesus.

We can realize the effects in this life of Christ's intercessory work, while looking forward to being with him throughout eternity, in addition to all the promises given for us in the scripture while here on earth.

The Table of Shewbread

Exodus 25: 23-30; Leviticus 24:5-7; Matthew 12:2-4;
John 6: 33-35

I.   Material and Size Wood and Gold

1½ feet by 2½ feet high by 3 feet long
1.   Typical Significance, Fellowship
2.   The Crown
3.   The Border

II. The unleavened Bread

1.   Made From Fine Flour
2.   Made Without Leaven

Supplement to Outline

"Behold, I stand at the door and knock: if any man hear my voice, and open the door, I will come in to him, and will sup with him. And he with me." (Revelation 3:20). Here we have the Lord Jesus Christ speaking concerning the conditions by which we have fellowship with Him. Namely, open the door of our heart.Many times, during Jesus's earthly ministry, we see him at the table with those whom he loved. He yearns to have fellowship and communion with us today. He is the bread of life. The invitation is, "Come and dine."

Here in the Tabernacle, we have the table before us. The priest could not sit at the table; it was too small. Even if he could have sat at the table, there was no chair or other provision for rest. The priest was always standing as he performed his duties.

The tenth chapter of Hebrews, verses 11-12, says, "And every priest stand daily ministering and offering oftentimes the same sacrifice, which can never take away sins: but this man (speaking of Jesus), after he had offered one sacrifice for sins forever, sat down on the right hand of God."

There is no rest for the human soul, except as we trust the finished work of our high priest, Christ Jesus, who is at the right hand of the Father. He is there to make intercession for whosoever will call upon him.

Only those who place their trust in the *Bread of Life—Jesus Christ*—can enjoy fellowship around this table. In other words, fellowship around this table is limited to believers only.

The Table of Shewbread was sufficiently large enough to support the twelve loaves of bread.

Fellowship

We are familiar with Psalm 23:5, "Thy prepares a table before me in the presence of mine enemies."

We are reminded of *The Lord's Supper* and how we are expected to remember the death of Jesus, as we partake.

The Crowns

These may well represent the exaltation of Jesus he was once crowned with a crown of thorns, but the time will come when he will be crowned king of kings.

The Border

The border surrounded the loaves of bread, and measured 4 ½ inches wide. We cannot clearly see the purpose of this border. It may have been provided to prevent the loaves from falling off the table. Surely it served to assist in some way. The border could illustrate for the many assets or helps available for our use in the study of God's Word. Commentaries, concordance, Bible history, history of the church, etc. Of course any of these should be used prayerfully.

The Twelve Loaves of Bread

This bread was not to contain any leaven or yeast. Leaven, in the scripture, is always a type of sin.

> Exodus 1:15;
>> Leviticus 2:11;
>>> Matthew 16:6;
>>>> Mark 8:15;
>>>>> 1 Corinthians 5:6-8;
>>>>> All of these teach this.

The unleavened bread speaks to us concerning the *Living Word of God—Jesus Christ*—who said, "I am the bread of life."

The Written Word

The Lord Jesus Christ chose twelve disciples, some of who wrote a large portion of the New Testament.

There was just the twelve loaves of bread on the table. The word "shewbread" means "presence bread" Perhaps so named because of the close proximity to the very presence of God in the Tabernacle. It was placed just before the Holy of Holies. Scripture states that this bread was made from fine flour. There was nothing course or undesirable about the flour. Again, this gives us a picture of Jesus Christ—the living word. Pontius Pilate said, "I find no fault in this man."

Flour

Flour in itself is anything but palatable. It must be subjected to fire before it can be appreciated. Hot bread is much more desirable than raw dough. The wheat for the flour must of necessity be crushed before it becomes usable for bread.

Without Leaven

The aspect of this bread is the most significant, concerning the priest relationship to it. The priest, regardless of his dignity or elected position, was required to partake of the bread.

Again, no matter who, the only way to God the Father is through *the Bread of Life—the Lord Jesus Christ.* It does not matter how good we might think we are—good neighbor, good spouse, good parent, good employee, good church person, etc. That will not do it. All must take the Lord Jesus Christ—the Living Word—the Bread of Life—into their heart for salvation. His righteousness imparted to us, which is the only righteousness that God will recognize.

The Inner Veil

Exodus 26:31-35, Matthew 27:50-51, Hebrews 10:20-21

I. The Un-Rent Veil

    1. Its place in the Tabernacle;
    2. Physical Characteristics: Material, Color, Cherubim;
    3. The Pillars.

II. The Rent Veil

    1. Its symbolical meaning;
    2. Its real significance;

        a. Man has access to the Throne of God
        b. God's invitation to come

Supplement to the Outline

The subject should stir our heart, perhaps as no other. We have before us a beautiful picture, and one most sacred heart searching. The Inner Vail was not just another veil or curtain. It was the innermost veil, with special significance, and of utmost importance.

The Inner Veil

First, let us bring out attention to the *un-rent veil* as it appeared intact, not only in the Tabernacle, but the temple itself.

The Inner Veil is a type of Jesus's human body. The scripture is very specific in respect to the typology here. Hebrews 10:20-21: "By a new and living way, which he hath consecrated for us, through the veil, that is to say, his flesh, and having a high priest over the house of God." With this truth in mind, we now see *"the un-rent veil"* as representing Jesus before he was crucified.

We see the veil as a barrier to the priest who daily ministered in the Holy Place. Only once a year could he enter into the Holy of Holies, into God's presence, that being on the Day of Atonement. The one single thing preventing admittance into the Holy of Holies was this Inner Veil. This was true until Jesus came in the flesh and finished his work. Before his death on the cross, man was unable to approach God. Except, the mediator of a God appointed priest.

The Veil's Place in the Tabernacle

As said before, the Inner Veil separated the Holy of Holies from the Holy Place. This was God's appointed place of worship. Still, we should be reminded that God does not dwell in such a place today. The Spirit of God in the church age is everywhere; the Holy Spirit is now dwelling in many tabernacles; tabernacles not made with hands. Question: Where are these tabernacles? 1 Corinthians 3:16-17: "Know ye not that the Spirit of God dwelleth in you? If any man defile the temple of God, him shall God destroy, for the temple of God is holy which temple ye are."

God is very jealous of his rightful place in our heart. To him, our heart is a sacred place of communion and fellowship. When we use the word "heart" here, it is not the organ that pumps the blood through our circulatory system, but is the inner man—*our most inner being.*

Physical Characteristics

The veil was made of Egyptian linen, pure white. Interwoven within were colors of blue, purple, and red, also woven into the veil were Cherubim; all speaking symbolically of Christ Jesus and the holiness of God.

The Pillars

The pillars were four in number, made of shittim wood overlaid with pure gold. These pillars differ in four ways from those at the court gate:

1. They were twice as long;
2. Were founded upon silver;
3. Were covered with gold rather than brass;
4. Were cut off at the top:

Could it be the veil pillars speak to us of Jesus in the four gospels? Just as the pillars were cut off, his life was cut off out of the land of the living. Isaiah 53:8: "He was taken from prison and from judgment: and who shall declare his generation? For he was cut off out of the land of the living: for the transgressions of my people was stricken."

The Rent Veil

Matthew 27:51: "and, behold, the veil of the temple was rent in twine, from top to bottom: and the earth did quake and the rocks rent."

As Jesus hung on the cross, committed himself into the Father's hands and gave up the ghost, the veil was rent from top to bottom, representing his flesh torn on the cross.

In John's gospel, Jesus repeatedly made the statement, "I lay down my life." While the cross was on the ground, Jesus willingly lay himself upon it. The Roman solders drove the nails through his hands and feet. While in agony, the solders lifted the cross in place.

Here, he hung between heaven and earth. Now dying to settle the sin question once and for all, he says, "*It is finished.*"

What does this mean to you and me today? Through his finished work, beside providing a perfect and complete salvation, we have immediate access to the throne of God.

The Ark of the Covenant

Exodus 25:10-22, Hebrews 9:4

    I.   Physical Characteristics, Size, and Material.

    II. Contents:

        1.   Tables of the Law;
        2.   Golden Pot of Manna;
        3.   Aaron's Rod that Budded;

    III. Relative Position:

        1.   In the Tabernacle;
        2.   On the Journey;

The ark contained three items: a pot of manna, Aaron's rod that budded, and the tablets of the Law; all depicted sin. The tablets of the Law were reminders of Israel's violation of God's authority; Aaron's rod that budded evidenced rejection of God's plan regarding the authority of the Levitical priesthood; and the pot of manna typifies man's rejection of divine provision.

Physical Characteristics, Size, and Material

While comparatively small, the ark nevertheless was a very valuable treasure chest. It was enhanced by a golden crown covered with a fine, beaten gold lid called *the Mercy Seat;* a part of this Mercy Seat were two Cherubim. The area immediately over the Ark was hallowed by God's presence. It was here that God had said, "*I will meet with thee.*"

The Ark was 3 feet 3 inches long, 2 feet 3 inches wide, and 2 feet 3 inches deep. A small piece of furniture, but very precious and sacred to Israel.

As Israel journeyed in the wilderness, the Ark was carried only on the shoulders of the priest, exalted and lifted up. Jesus said, "If I be lifted up I will draw all men to me."

No one was supposed to touch the Ark, with exception of the priest. If anyone else did so, they would die.

Golden Pot of Manna

There is little doubt that this manna given to the Israelites by Jehovah God, as they traveled through the wilderness, is a type of the Lord Jesus Christ.

John 6:32-33: "Verily, verily, I say unto you, Moses gave you not that bread from heaven, but my Father giveth you the bread from heaven. For the bread of God is he which cometh down from heaven, and giveth life unto the world."

Aaron's Rod

Was simply a dead lifeless piece of wood. In the seventeenth chapter of Numbers, it came alive, budded, blossomed, brought forth fruit (almonds). We have nothing less than life from the dead; Jesus was resurrected from the dead! Hear him say, "I am the resurrection and the life: he that believeth in me, though he were dead, yet shall he live" (John 11:25).

Then John 14:19: "Because I live, ye shall live also."

The Position of the Ark

The ark was located in the Holy of Holies, just beyond the Altar of Incense. However, the veil stood as a barrier between the two.

Today, our prayers are close to the throne of God without a barrier, because of Jesus's death on the cross; through him, we can come boldly to the Throne of God.

On the Journey

The Ark was in the midst of the Israelite as they journeyed. Just as the Ark was where it was needed most, among the people, so is Christ Jesus, and more than willing to help in time of need. He is more than ready to lead than we are to follow. If we fail to follow, it is sure not his fault.

Where is the ark today? Where are all those valuable and sacred treasures? We only know that it was carried away many years ago into Babylon during the captivity. For sure, it is no longer on a journey. Neither is Jesus, he is now preparing a place for whosoever, waiting for the Father to give the command once more to leave his heavenly place and receive his own for himself.

The Mercy Seat, Cherubim, and Shekinah Glory

Exodus 25:17-22, Leviticus 16:2, Psalm 80:1

   I. The Mercy Seat.

      1. A Meeting Place.
      2. A Resting Place.
      3. A Place *of* Mercy.
      4. A Throne.

  II. Cherubim.

      1. Their Purpose.
      2. Their Attitude.

 III. Shekinah Glory.

Supplement to the Outline

The Mercy Seat and Cherubim consisted of one integral unit made from solid, beaten gold. The only other article within the Tabernacle similarly constructed was the candlestick.

In respect to the material here, we do not find the presence of wood. We do not find humanity represented in any way. This place of mercy was conceived and wrought by God.

We shall find in the discussion, the Shekinah Glory representing the very presence of God and the cloud that veiled his presence. This cloud led his people, Israel, through the wilderness. Today, the Holy Spirit leads his people.

Exodus 25:21-22: "And thou shalt put the mercy seat above the ark; and in the ark thou shalt put the testimony that I shall give thee.

"And there I will meet with thee, and I will commune with thee from above the mercy seat, from between the two cherubim which are upon the ark of the testimony, of all things which I give thee in commandment unto the children of Israel."

Mercy Seat: Let Us Analyze These Words

There is a word found in the New Testament that gives us essentially the basic meaning. *Propitiation*, "and he is the propitiation for our sins: and not for ours only, but also for the sins of the whole world" (1 John 2:2).

Then in Romans 3:25: "Whom God hath set forth to be a propitiation through faith in his blood, to declare his righteousness for remission of sins that are past, through the forbearance of God."

The root meaning of *Mercy Seat* (hil-as-ter-ion) as found in Hebrews 9:5 has the same meaning as the word "propitiation," which is found both in the old and new covenant.

Mercy Seat and Cherubim consisted of one integral unit made from solid, beaten gold. In respect to the material, we do not find the presence of wood. Humanity is not represented in any way.

Just as the name implies, the Mercy Seat was a place of mercy. God had said that he would meet with his people here.

According to Leviticus Chapter 16, once a year, on the Day of Atonement, the High Priest entered the Holy of Holies, sprinkled the Mercy Seat with blood from the Brazen Altar. As a result, God was merciful to his people and the High Priest and postponed judgment for sin.

The Meeting Place was the place where God met with his people, suspended judgment for sin until his Son Jesus Christ should come and pay the sin debt with his blood.

The Crowns at the edge of the Mercy Seat did more than enhance. They speak of Christ's exaltation. His Royal Rightness or Kingship. Jesus, though rejected by the Jews, will reign as king of kings and lord of lords.

A Place of Resting: Where else in the world today can you find rest for your soul? Certainly, in this time of squandering, grasping for pleasure age, we need an anchor that is steadfast and sure; we need a resting place. That place can be found in Jesus. In the eleventh chapter of Matthew, he says, "Come unto me all ye that labor and are heavy laden, and I will give you rest. Take my yoke upon you, and learn of me: for I am meek and lowly in heart, and ye shall find rest unto your souls. For my yoke is easy, and my burden is light."

Cherubim: The Cherubim look down upon the blood-sprinkled Mercy Seat, covering it with their wings. Their attitude toward this indicates God's value placed on the blood sprinkles of the Mercy Seat. Our attitude the blood of Jesus has been expressed by the Apostle Peter.

1 Peter 1:18-19:

18. For as much as ye know that ye were not redeemed with corruptible things, as silver and gold, from vain conversation received by tradition from your fathers.
19. But with the precious blood of Christ, as a lamb without blemish and without spot.

Shekinah Glory

This is an untranslated word, meaning, "There will I meet with you" was at the Mercy Seat that was sprinkled with the blood that God came down and met with his people in his Shekinah Glory.

Today, there is no approach, no Mercy Seat, or any other salvation other than through a personal recognition of the effectiveness of the blood of Jesus and a personal exercise of simple faith in his shed blood. This is the basis of New Testament doctrine, and there is no substitute for it.

The High Priest

Exodus 28, Hebrews 7:24-25, 8:1-2, 1 John 2:1-2

The Ephod: Color and Material: Gold, Blue, Purple, Scarlet, and White;
Curious Girdle of the Ephod;
Onyx Stones: The Engraved Names;
Breastplate of Judgment.—

The Precious Stones;
Urim and Thummim

The Robe;
Golden Plate;
The Coat;
The Miter.

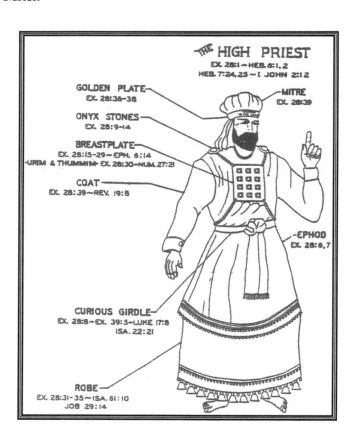

The High Priest

Introduction

In the beginning, man acted as his own priest. God the Father dealt directly with Adam and Eve. Cain and Abel offered their own sacrifices to God.

Later, we find that the head of the household offering sacrifice to God for himself and his household.

Still later, men chose of God as mediator or priest for man and nation.

Finally, Jesus Christ, himself, as priest for the entire world. He said, "No man cometh to the Father but by me." Today, the only way man can reach God the Father is through Jesus Christ. He is our only mediator.

The scripture identifies the Christian as one who is a priest.

Revelation 1:5-6: "from Jesus Christ, who is the faithful witness, and the first begotten of the dead, unto him that Loved us and washed us from our sins in his own blood and hath made us kings and priest unto God and his Father."

Today, the believer is acting as priest for the unsaved. The believer's prayers of intercession on behalf of the lost is certainly his sacred duty and responsibility, even greater than any former priest.

Aaron was commissioned by Jehovah God to serve as High Priest for the nation of Israel (Exod. 28:1; Heb. 5:4,10).

He was not only called, but was cleansed in order to be properly prepared to perform his sacred duties (Exod. 29:1).

As high priest of Israel, he was immaculately clothed with God's righteousness, and consecrated by God for his service (Exod. 29:5-6-7).

Even so, we, as believers in Christ, are clothed with his righteousness and consecrated by God for his service. Isaiah 61:10: "I will greatly rejoice in the Lord, my soul shall be joyful in my God, for he hath clothed me with the garments of salvation, he hath covered me with the robe of righteousness, as a bride groom decketh himself with ornaments, and as a bride adorneth herself with jewels."

See Aaron a Type of Jesus Christ as High Priest

There are many reference to this in the scripture, particularly in the book Hebrews, beginning with chapter three.

While Jesus is a priest after the order of Melchizedek, he executes his office after the pattern of Moses. In Hebrews chapter seven, we have the order given; in chapter nine, we have the pattern.

Aaron's high priest work was only a shadow of what Jesus Christ came to do and can do now for whosoever.

Hebrews 7:25: "Wherefore, he is able also to save them to the uttermost that come unto God by him, seeing he ever liveth to make intersession for them."

Aaron was both compassionate and a compassed high priest (Heb. 5:1-2).

Jesus also is both of these and more. How many times do we read in the scripture and he was moved by compassion? Also, Jesus was commissioned by God the Father to come into the world on behalf of mankind, and Jesus has commissioned all believers to go teach the gospel to all nations, baptizing in the name of the Father, and the Son, and the Holy Ghost (Matt. 28:19).

Let us now observe the attire of the high priest;

The Ephod (E-Pod)

It was worn by Aaron and his successors as they performed their priestly duties in the Holy Place. This was an outer garment of linen and gold. The color speaks in the same significant way we have found them to represent them through the Tabernacle.

In additional to the typical truth already given, it is interesting to know that the color of blue and red when mingled together produce purple, the color of royalty.

The Girdle Denotes Service or Action

We gather this somewhat from the "spiritual armor" given to us in Ephesians 6:13-18. Here, we are admonished, among other things, to gird ourselves with "the truth" and put on the whole armor of God, ready to do battle against the Devil when he comes against us.

The girdle appears to be an integral part of the Ephod. Therefore, represents Jesus ready as servant of man.

The Onyx Stones

These were placed on the shoulders of the priest. Shoulders are for bearing burdens.

The priests were to bear the burdens of the twelve tribes of Israel. These engraved stones were a divine reminder of this.

Jesus Christ, as our High Priest, is our burden bearer. Our names are also written down; not on the shoulders of Jesus, but in the *Lamb's Book of Life*.

The names of the twelve tribes of Israel were engraved in the onyx stones, speaking of our common ground for salvation.

The names were engraved in chronological order, according to birth (Exod. 28:10).

Our name are written in "The Lamb's Book of Life" because of our new birth (John 3:7).

The Breastplate of Judgement

We are told that the name literally means "Ornament of Decision."

While in the Old Testament, we have "The Breastplate of Judgement"; we find in the New Testament "The Breastplate of Righteousness" (Eph. 28:10).

The Breastplate of Judgment worn by the priest was foursquare as the Brazen Altar.

The Precious Stones

The breastplate displays these twelve stones, set in pure gold, placed uniformly in rows. Not only do we have here a picture of Israel close to the heart of God, but believers in Christ as well. Just as the precious stones were set in the gold breastplate, so we in Christ, placed there by God himself (John 15:16).

Just as there was one breastplate with many jewels, so is there one Christ but many believers.

In the interest of brevity, we shall tabulate herein each jewel specifically and subsequent related data pertinent to these jewels.

Given along with the tribal name you will find the meaning of each:

Jewel	Tribe	Tribal Characteristics	
Sardius Predominantly red	Judah (Praise)	The tribe through whom Christ came.	Red representing the blood sacrifice of Christ.
Topaz (Brilliant yellow Topaz means "to seek"	Issachar (Reward)	A cheerful people	The yellow may represent cheerfulness, having received a reward after diligently seeking.

Carbuncle A Glittering Jewel Color unknown	Zebulum (Dwelling)	Served as a haven for ships (Gen. 49:13)	This tribe perhaps served the same purpose as harbor lights today.
Emerald Sea Green	Emerald (See a son)	Like the troubled sea—unstable, very sinful	
Sapphire Second hardest stone known.	Simeon (Hearing)	Hard and ruthless	
Diamond Hardest of all stones	Gad (A troop)	Great warriors	1 Chronicles 5:18
Ligure Characteristics Obscure	Ephraim (Very fruitful)	Youngest son of Joseph	
Agate Reflects its beauty only when split. A semi-translucent compound mineral	Manasseh (Forgetting)	The tribe of Manasseh was divided	Oldest son of Joseph
Amethyst Purple	Benjamin (Son of my right hand)	The smallest tribe. A warring tribe.	Christ is the Son of the Father's right hand.
Beryl Meaning to break or subdue	Dan (Judge)	Led Israel into idolatry	Judges 19:30, 31
Onyx Fire-like—very brilliant and very precious	Asher (Blessed)	Genesis 49:20	
Jasper Clear as crystal Sometimes bright yellow (Rev. 21:10, 11)	Naphtali (My wrestlings)	Freedom-loving	Genesis 49:21

The tribes of Joseph and Levi were not inscribed upon the breastplate. Joseph was represented by his two sons Manasseh and Ephraim.

Joseph, which means "fruitful," was born because God himself had intervened (Gen. 30:22-24).

He became a perfect type of Jesus Christ.

The name "Levi" means "joined closely." This tribe was set apart to perform the rites associated with the Tabernacle Worship.

U-Rim and Thummim (thim-mim):

These words mean "*light* and *perfection.*"

The Robe

This is the first time we find a robe mentioned in the scripture. The robe worn by the priest was blue and had attached to the hem golden bells and pomegranates. Blue throughout the Tabernacle speak of the *divine heavenly one*, of whom the high priest as only of type. The pomegranates were blue, purple, and scarlet, the same significant color elsewhere.

On the Day of Atonement, none of the beautiful garments were worn. On this day, only the white garments were worn. This was a day of humiliation; a picture of the sinner coming for salvation.

The Coat

It was of fine linen and cunning embroider. It was an extraordinary coat. It is well to remember that there is nothing ordinary about God's plan for salvation.

The Miter

Only the high priest wore the miter. The other priest wore bonnets (Exod. 28:39-40).

Both were made of fine linen. Both were coverings for the head. This in itself is a symbol of obedience to a higher order today, "The Church Age," "The Sixth Dispensation OF Time." 1 Timothy 2:5 declares there is one God and one mediator between God and man; that mediator, Christ Jesus, "*our High Priest.*"

Jesus was both God and man. Jesus Christ as man. Christ Jesus as God. Therefore, can mediate to God for man. Man himself can never accomplish this, no matter who he may be.

CHAPTER NINE

Leaving Mt. Sinai

Numbers 10:11-12: "And it came to pass on the twentieth day of the second month, in the second year, that the cloud was taken up from off the tabernacle of the testimony, and the children of Israel took their journey out of the wilderness of Sinai."

When the Tabernacle was finished, a cloud covered the tent of the congregation, and the glory of the Lord filled the Tabernacle.

In Genesis, God spoke from heaven;
In Exodus, he spoke from the mountain;
In Leviticus, he spoke from the tabernacle;
Leviticus gives the law for the walk, service, and worship for redeemed people.

The book of Numbers covers the final preparation for going into the promised land.

The Israelites had spent about one year at Mt. Sinai. This was a scared place to them. Here, God had given them the law and had entered into a covenant with them.

A Census Is Taken

The first numbering, not counting the Levites, was made of all the male of Israel from twenty years old and upward. There were 603,550 of them. The second numbering was of all the male of the tribe of Levi. This numbering was from one-month-old upward. There were twenty-two thousand of them.

The Levites were to do all the work of the Tabernacle, were to have charge of all the vessels, and were in charge of moving and setting up of the Tabernacle. No one but the Levite were to come into the Tabernacle. If they did, they would be put to death. You see, God wants a separate people to do his work.

The Levites were the ones that God chose to give to Aaron and his sons, that they might be ministers of taking care of the Tabernacle. God could do this because he owned them.

The first born had belonged to him ever since the death of the first born in Egypt. He now chose to trade them, so, a third numbering took place. The numbering followed the same as that of the Levites; all males from one-month-old and upward. There were 22,273. God was going to release 273 more first born than he was going to receive. They must buy their release. The redemption was five shekels, $3.25 per person, a total of $887. 25. This money was to be paid to Aaron who was God's representative.

Nothing was done by chance. No one did their own thing. Their place in the line was designated. Their place in the camp was designated. Their work was planned and organized by God. Now everything was in order. The cloud rises.

They took down their tents, packed their belongings on the backs of their donkeys, collected their flocks, and resumed their journey. They carefully dismantled and packed the sanctuary as well. Then they placed the sacred Ark of the ovenant on two long poles, which the priest carried at the head of the caravan.

The Main Events of the Journey

Slowly, they made their way northward toward Canaan. Several weeks later, they came to the wilderness of Param—a forbidding chalk and limestone plateau, stretching for about eight miles along the eastern edge of the Sinai Peninsula.

They had not been long on the way when they began to complain about the way. This displeased God; his anger was kindled, fire fell, and many were consumed (Num. 11:1).

They cried out to Moses; Moses prayed to God; and the fire was quenched.

Next, they complained for food. This complaining was started by the mixed multitude. Israel soon took it up. Day after day, they complained of hunger. "We remember the fish we ate in Egypt for nothing, the cucumbers, the melons, the leaks, the onions, and the garlic, but now our strength is dried up. There is nothing at all but this manner."

Exasperated, Moses went off by himself and cried out to God. Why had he had to carry the responsibility of all these people? Ask God to let him die—to be free of this burden. God answered, but not in a way Moses asked. God gave him instruction to gather seventy elders and bring them to the tabernacle of the congregation; they were to stand there with him.

Numbers 11:17: ". . . I will come down and will talk with thee there: and I will take of the Spirit which is upon thee, and put it upon them; and they shall bear the burden of the people with thee, that thou bear it not alone."

Nothing is said of any more Spirit being added; it was just spread over them. It does not take any more of the Spirit of God to get the job done. He just needs someone to use.

The complaint of the people was answered. Numbers 11:31: "And there went forth a wind from the Lord, and brought quail from the sea, and let them fall on the camp . . . ," and goes on to say, "all that night and the next day they gathered quail. While they ate the wrath of the Lord was kindled against the people. The Lord smote them with a very great plague. Many of them were buried there. From here they move on to Hazeroth."

The Rebellion of Miriam and Aaron

Numbers 12:1: "And Miriam and Aaron spoke against Moses because of the Egyptian woman whom he had married." Then in verse 2, ". . . hath the Lord indeed spoke only to Moses? Hath he not spoken also to us?" The Lord was very displeased with this. He came down in the pillar of the cloud, stood at the door of the Tabernacle, called Miriam and Aaron, and they came forth, to listen to what God says to them, "Hear now my words: If there be a prophet among you, I the Lord will make myself known unto him in a vision, and will speak unto him in a dream. My servant Moses is not so, who is faithful in all mine house. With him I speak mouth to mouth, even apparently, and not in dark speeches; and the similitude of the Lord shall behold. Wherefore then were ye not afraid to speak against my servant Moses?"

The anger of the Lord was kindled against them, and he departed. But that was not the end of it. The cloud departed from off the Tabernacle, and Miriam was leprous, white as snow. Moses cried out to the Lord. Miriam was shut out from the camp for seven days, the restored well.

Now the caravan laves Hazeroth and reach the edge of the wilderness, stop at Kadesh, a large oasis just north of Paran. Here, they are only fifty miles away from the southern border of Canaan.

Spies Sent to Canaan

Numbers 13:1-2: "And the Lord spake unto Moses, saying, Send thou men, that they may search the land of Canaan, of every tribe of the fathers shall send a man, every one a ruler among them."

Moses chose the twelve men to spy out the land. He gave the instruction, "Go up unto the hill country, and see what the land is, whether the people that dwell there in it are they strong or weak, whether they are few or many, whether the land thy dwell in is good or bad, whether the cities that they dwell in are camps or strong hold, whether there is wood in it or not. Be of good courage, and bring back some of the fruit of the land."

The mission took forty days. Upon their return, the people were assembled to hear their report. All twelve agreed that it was a good land, highly desirable to them. Ten reported they could not size the land; it was a walled city with great fighting men. Two, Joshua and Caleb, reported it could be done, saying, "Let us go up at once and possess it for we are well able to overcome (Num. 13:30).

But the majority was not willing to undertake the conquest.

This lack of faith, when every reason they should have trusted God, who had so often delivered them. In God's eye, it was a grievous sin and must be punished. With the exception of Joshua and Caleb, every one of the generation above twenty years of age would die before they came to the land of promise. All that had come out of Egypt would now wander in the wilderness for years.

The ten spies that had the bad report were instantly killed by a plague (Num. 14:36).

Complain of the Leaders

Next they complain about their leaders. They said, since God was among all of them, Moses and Aaron had no more authority than any of the others. They implied that the tribe of Ruben should be the leaders of Israel because he was the elder son of Jacob when it seemed that they were ready to overturn the spiritual, as well as the civil leadership of Israel. Moses prayed to God. God answered with a plague that fourteen thousand and seven Hundred died (Num. 16:49).

The Authority of Aaron Is Established

Numbers 17:1-13: A leader from each tribe was to bring a rod, and Moses to place them in the Tabernacle. God said to Moses in verse five, "and it shall be that the rod of the man whom I choose will blossom: thus I will rid myself of the complains of the children of Israel which they make against me."

The next day, when Moses went into the Tabernacle, Aaron's rod had sprouted and put forth buds, produced blossoms, yielded ripe almonds. Aaron's rod had gone beyond the requirement of the test—a strong affirmation of his authority.

Numbers Chapter 18: The Lord addressed three speeches to Aaron, and one to Moses.

The first speech, verses 1-7, answer the question of the people in 17:13, namely, how the people can avoid death when they are bringing sacrifices to the Tabernacle; the other speeches deal with the support of the priest and the Levites, since they will receive no allotment of the land.

To Moses, basely, the Lord spake to him concerning the tithe and the heave offering. Of the tithes received, was to offer up a tenth part of the tithe to Aaron. Was to give him the best. Was counted to the Levites as increase. Could be eaten because, for it was received for their services in the Tabernacle.

Miriam's Death

When they came into the land of Zin at Kadesh, Miriam died and was buried there.

There was no water there; again, the people complained. Moses and Aaron went to the door of the Tabernacle, fell on their faces. The glory of the Lord appeared unto them.

Numbers 20:7-8: "And the Lord spake unto Moses, saying, Take thy rod, and gather the assembly together, thou, and Aaron thy brother, and speak ye unto the rock before their eyes: and it shall give forth water."

Moses's Great Mistake

Moses and Aaron assembled the people before a large rock, weary and impatient at the constant complaining. Moses says, "Hear now ye rebels, must we bring you water out of this rock?" He is lifting up himself and Aaron as though they could accomplish this miracle themselves. What does he do? Instead of speaking to the rock, he strikes the rock with his staff. Not once, but twice he strikes it. Water gushes out; the people and their cattle drink their fill.

Now the Lord says to Moses and Aaron, "Because you did not believe me you shall not bring the assembly into the land which I have given them."

When they come to Mt. Hor, Aaron dies and is buried there. Moses removed the official priestly robe and placed it on Eleazar, Aaron's son. The people observed a period of thirty days mourning and then resumed their journey.

When King Arod, the Canaanite, which dwelt in the south, heard that Israel came by the way of the spies, he fought against Israel, took some of them as prisoners. Israel made a vow unto the Lord, and said, "If thou wilt indeed deliver this people into my hand, then I will utterly destroy their cities." The Lord harkened to them and delivered up the Canaanites (Num. 21:1-3).

Now they journeyed from Mt. Hor by the way of the Red sea. The people were very weary discouraged and spake against Moses (Num. 21:5).

As a result of this, the Lord sent fiery serpents among the people. Many were bitten and died. As usual, they cried out to Moses:

"We have sinned, for we have spoken against the Lord, and against thee; pray unto the Lord, that he take away the serpents from us" (Num. 21:7).

Moses prayed; God gave him instruction to make a serpent and put it on a pole. Moses made a serpent of brass, places it on a pole, held it up; all those that look on it would live.

East of Jordan, this territory was won from Sihon, Og, the Moabites, and the Midianites. It was a very fertile land—very desirable for pasture, good for agriculture. When the conquest was won, the tribes of Reuben, Gad, and part of the tribe of Manassah, who were primarily interested in sheep raising, requested Moses to settle her as part of the promised land. Permission was granted, provided the fighting men of their tribes would cross Jordan and contribute their share in the task of conquering the future home of the other tribes.

CHAPTER TEN

Moses's Final Days

Before his final departure, there were some things Moses had to do. Among these, setting up the boundary of the Promised Land and giving final instruction to Joshua. It must have been a bitter disappointment to Moses to be punished so severely. But he accepted his fate without question.

With a heavy heart, he gathered his people together for the final leg of his journey. Now they move on and camp at Oboth, from Oboth to Ijeabarim, from here in the valley of Zared, then on the other side of Arnon, which is the wilderness that cometh out of the coast of the Amorites. From Arnon is the border of Moab. From scripture, the people of Moab and Eden were related to the Israelites. The Mobites were decadence of Moab, the son of Lot, grandnephew of Abraham. The Edimites were decadence of Esau, the hairy brother of Jacob.

For this reason, Moses might have thought they would let them pass through the two kingdoms in peace. But the king of Edom refused to grant permission for them to travel through his land. Unwilling to go to war about the matter, Moses led the people through a wide canyon along Edom's western border. Reaching the southern border of Moab, Moses sent to the king for permission to enter his country. Again, his request was denied. So they were forced to bypass Moab. Marching through the desolate wilderness to the east was the Arabian Desert.

At the northern frontier of Moab, the caravan finally turned westward toward Canaan. But still another obstacle lay in their path. Sihon, king of the territory directly north of Moab, also refused to let them pass through their land and sent an army to stop them. Finally forced to battle, the Israelites defeated Sihon's army. Now they continued their journey westward, continued gradually upward, across the limestone plateau. Climbing the high ridge of the plateau, they caught their first glimpse of the Jordan River and the land of Canaan beyond.

Their voices rang out in praise to the Lord as they began their decent to the plains of Moab. Here, they pitched their tents and began their final preparation to enter Canaan. Moses could not share wholehearted with their joy, for he knew his journey was coming to an end and that he would soon die.

Moses's Farewell Message

Sadly, Moses calls the people together and speaks to them for the last time. Of all the people who left Egypt, there were only three left, Moses, Joshua, and Caleb. For various reasons all of the others died on the journey. Now this young generation gathered around their beloved leader.

Now see Moses here. The man who stood before them was very old; his hair very white, his face and hands learn with age; the long years of wandering, the endless bickering, the disappointment, the burden and responsibility, all had their impact. Yet his eyes still flashed with a youthful spirit, and his words had force and conviction.

Slowly, he speaks to this young generation, telling them of the fight from Egypt, the pilgrimage to Mt. Sinai, how the law was given, and building of the Tabernacle and its purpose.

This is why we have the book of Deuteronomy, which means, *second giving of the Law*. The older generation had failed in teaching this young generation. Now Moses is speaking all the words that God had spoke to him at Mt. Sinai. (The book of Deuteronomy is quoted from thirty-five times in the New Testament.) Moses urged this young generation to keep the commandment of "The Lord Your God," "Loving the Lord Your God," and *"walking in his ways, and his statues of his ordinances"* was his words.

Then he says to them, "Then ye shall live and multiply, and the Lord your God will bless you in the land which you are entering to take possession of it."

Then he warns them, "But if your heart turns away and drawn away to worship other Gods and serve them, I declare unto you this day that ye shall perish."

He pauses, takes a good look at the attentive young faces looking toward him. Then he continues, "I am 120 years old this day. I am no longer able to go out and come in. The Lord has said unto me, ye shall not go over Jordan. The Lord your God himself will go over before you, so that you shall dispossess them. Joshua will go over at your head as the Lord hath spoken."

When he had finished speaking, he picks up his staff, turns, and leaves. He walks alone across the plain to the foot of Mount Nebo. Slowly, he climbs up the steep rocky mass, higher and higher, until he reaches the summit.

Looking back, he could see his people camped far below him on the plain. The sun is beginning to sink out of sight. He could see the flickering lights of the camp fires. His eyes came to rest on the Tabernacle. Smoke is rising in black clouds from the Brazen Altar where priests are sacrificing a lamb.

Reluctantly, he turns and looks westward; out over the far side of the mountain, there is the light of the setting sun; the land of Canaan lays directly below. He could see the fertile green valley of the Jordan River; to the south, he could see the waters of the Dead Sea glimmering red and gold in the sunset and there the Jordan hill, rising steeply westward toward Jerusalem. His eyes fall on the winding course of the Jordan River, northward to the blue waters of the Sea of Galilee. The last rays of sunlight disappear. He closes his eyes, with the image of the Promise Land still before him; the great man dies. Somewhere in the hill country lay his body.

The life of Moses is told in the books of Exodus, Leviticus, Numbers, and Deuteronomy. There has not a prophet since in Israel like Moses. None like him for all the signs and wonders which the Lord sent him to do in the land of Egypt, to Pharaoh and to all his servants and all the land, for all the mighty power and all the great deeds which Moses wrought in the sight of Israel.

CHAPTER ELEVEN

Entering Canaan

Joshua 1:2-3: God is speaking to Joshua:

1. Moses my servant is dead: now therefore arise, go over this Jordan, thou and all this people into the land which I do give them, even the children of Israel.
2. Every place that the sole of your feet shall tread upon, that have I given unto you, as I said to Moses.

Joshua had served successfly under Moses; he had followed well. Now his status changed. Now he must carry the responsibility. It is apparent that the people accepted and followed him with confidence. They are now in the hands of a new leader—one younger and less experienced than Moses, but one who trusted Jehovah and sought with all his power to measure up to his heavy responsibilities.

Picture here, Joshua standing with bowed head, lonely heart. His counselor and friend is dead. Now God speaks to him. God's command is seasoned with promise:

> "You go, I will go with you."
> "You fight, I will fight with you."

"No man shall be able to stand before you: as I was with Moses, so shall I be with you, have faith, be not afraid, be strong and courageous, observe and do all the law, be not afraid neither be thou dismayed, for the Lord thy God is with thee wheresoever thou goest" (Josh. 1:5-9).

What God is saying Joshua is, "If you do as instructed, everything will go well."

In verse eight, Joshua is admonished to know the law and to meditate upon it day and night. This is why some fail, not knowing the scripture—*the Word of God.*

We have to know something before we can meditate upon it. In these difficult days, the truth is sandwiched between fanaticism and modernism. To find the truth, we must fast, pray, and study, and the pray some more. God's Word is a lamp unto our feet and the light unto our path.

Joshua, a prince of the tribe of Ephriam, and Caleb, prince of the tribe of Judah, were the only two of the twelve spies that Moses sent into Canaan with a good report and favored an attack at that time.

Now time had come; in preparation for the invasion, Joshua sends two spies into the city of Jericho. Under the cover of night, they cross the plains of Moab, forded the rushing waters of the Jordan River. Swiftly, they traveled to Jordan valley approaching Jericho in the gray morning light. They had no trouble slipping through the gateway and entering the town unnoticed. They found lodging at the house of a harlot named Rahab. Since she was custom to receiving strange men, their presence would not have aroused curiosity. Rahab's house, like many others in Jericho, was built into the wall of the city. From there, the spies had a good vantage point from which they could view the city and evaluate the strength of its resistance.

Before dawn the next morning, the spies wandered through the crooked, narrow streets. What they saw would have been very strange to them. Along the eastern street ran a clay trench, designed for drainage of water and sewage. Makeshift, one-story houses made of mud brick huddled side by side at the streets edge. In the midst, stood the two-story palace of the king and his chapel—a temple of Buddah.

When the spies returned to Rahab's house, she hid them among the stalks of flax that was drying on her roof. She advised them to wait until evening to make their escape.

Someone must have noticed their presence; because late that day, solders had come to Rahab's door, demanded that she hand over the spies to them. She said, "Two men came to me, but I did not know where they came from, and when the gate was to be closed, at dark, the men went out. Where the men went I do not know, but if you pursue them quickly, you will overtake them."

The solders hurried away. Rahab climbed up to the rooftop and told the spies what had happened. Bewildred, they ask her why she had taken such a great risk to save them. Listen to what she says to the, "I know that the Lord has given you the land, and that the fear of you has fallen upon us, and that all the inhabitants of the land melt away before you. For we have heard how he divided up the waters of the Red Sea before you when you came out of Egypt, and what you did to the Amorites that were beyond Jordan. Sihon and Og. As soon as we heard it, our hearts melted, and there was no courage left in any man because of you. For the Lord your God, he is God of heaven above, and in the earth below. Now therefore I pray you, swear unto me by the Lord, since I have shown you kindness that ye will also show kindness unto my fathers house and give a true token that ye will save alive my father and my mother, my brethren, and my sisters, and all that they have, an deliver our lives from death" (Josh. 2:9-13).

The two spies, in gratitude for the valuable help and information, agreed to what she asked.

With a scarlet rope, she lowered them down from her house, cautioned them to hide in the nearby hills for three days to be sure they would not be arrested by the kings solders.

The spies instructed her to bring her family to her house and place the scarlet rope in the window. Verse 21, she said, "According to your words, so be it."

After three days, the spies returned across the Jordan river with an encouraging report, "Truly the Lord has given all the land unto our hands, and moreover all the inhabitants of the land are faint hearted because of us."

At once Joshua gives orders, "Sanctify yourselves, for tomorrow the Lord will do wonders among us." At last, after bitter years of bondage and wilderness, and hardship, ahead of them was their future home, the Promised Land.

At dawn, the officers passed through the camp, ordering all to watch the Ark and follow it at a distance of two thousand cubits—three-quarters of a mile.

See the lesson here. We can share with the Lord in service as workers with him, but we can never lead him, we are supposed to be followers.

In the wilderness, they had followed the cloud by day and the pillar of fire by night. Now they would follow the Ark of the Covenant, which represented the presence of God.

Crossing the Jordan River

At God's command, Joshua told the people to follow the priest carrying the Ark. The priest was to step into the Jordan river and stand there while the people crossed over.

When the children of Israel left Egypt, with one stroke of Moses's hand, the waters parted, they marched over; a picture of salvation. Now, when it came to entering Canaan, it was a step by step walking into the water. This was a walk of faith.

It took great courage for the priest to step into the rushing water, but when the priest's feet touched the water, the waters rolled back. Joshua 3:16: "rose up in a heap."

With the opening of the water, the priest moved to the center of the riverbed and held the Ark while the people passed by them to cross to the other side of Jordan River. When the crossing was complete and the priest came upon the western bank, the waters came rolling down and overflowed the banks. So, on the tenth day of the first month of 1410 BC, they crossed Jordan.

To commemorate this crossing, twelve chief men, one from each tribe, brought from the bed of the river, twelve large stones with which they built a memorial on the western side of the river. They placed the stones in a circle and named the place *Gilgal,* which means *circle of stones.*

Joshua speaks to the children of Israel,

Joshua 4:21-24: "When your children shall ask their fathers in time to come, saying, What meaneth these stones? Then ye shall let your children know, saying, Israel came over the Jordan on dry land, that all the people of the earth may know the hand of Jehovah your God forever. They made Gilgal their military headquarters. Then on the fourteenth day, they kept the Passover. On the fifteenth day, the manna ceased to come. Now they were to eat the fruit of the land."

Their First Challenge

Jericho, sometimes called, "City of Palm Trees" is their first challenge. This walled city set in a beautiful surrounding, with fertile planes, and springs of water. Later would be called "Elisha's Springs" (2 Kings 2:19-20).

The city was famous for its balsam trees, which produced a balm known for its healing qualities. In Joshua's time, a beautiful forest of palm trees some eight miles long and three miles wide stood immediately east of the city. Jericho was almost concealed between the steep hills on the west side and the forest on the east. It was a major Canaanite city, devoted to the moon god.

Since it was practically impossible to get to the western highlands by any other route, Jericho must be conquered if they were ever to succeed in taking their homeland. It would be fatal to leave such a fortified city in the hands of their enemies.

Meanwhile, the people of Jericho had detected the Israelites encampment. Joshua 6:1: "Now Jericho was straitly shut up because of the children of Israel: none went out, and none came in."

Joshua's Faith in Action

Joshua 6:2: "And the Lord said to Joshua, I have given unto thine hand Jericho, and the king thereof, and the mighty one of Value."

To say the least, Israel's siege on Jericho was unconventional. Seven priests were to take up the "Ark of the Covenant." Bearing seven trumpets of Ram's horn, the armed men were to go before them, all the other people following the priest, marching around the city. For six days, they were to march around the city, and on the seventh day, they were to march around the city seven times. Joshua's command to them was: They were not to make any noise with their voice, "neither shall any word proceed out of your mouth until I bid you shout." On the seventh day, when they had marched around the city seven times, the priests were to blow the trumpets, and when the people heard the loud blast of the trumpets and Joshua gave the command to shout, they were to shout with a loud voice. The walls of the city would fall down flat. They were to go into the city and destroy everything in it—men, women, children, and animals. Only Rahab and her family were to be spared. No one was to keep anything for themselves. The silver, gold, and vessels of brass and iron were to be put in the treasury of the Lord.

This was the first city that God was to give them. We can well understand God requiring that they should devote the very first to him.

When God told Joshua he had given the city of Jericho into his hands, this did not mean that Joshua and the children of Israel could sit back and relax while the city automatically became theirs. They had something to do, and God had given them explicit instructions how to go about doing it. But they had to believe the Word of the Lord, and act upon it. Acting on God's Words was their faith in action.

Jericho Is Taken

Joshua 6:15:_ "And it came to pass on the seventh day, they rose up early about the dawn of the day, and compassed the city, after the manner seven times."

It must have been terrible on the nerves of the people of Jericho as they appeared day after day for six days in total silence, then on the seventh day, marching seven times. At the command, the priest blew the trumpets. Joshua says, "'Shout for the Lord has given you the city.' Only Rahab and those in her household were to be left alive."

Note: They were to shout while the walls were still up. Anyone can shout when the walls are down. That is not faith. They acted their faith, shouted with a great shout, and the walls fell flat.

The people went into the city and took it, utterly destroyed it—both men and women, children, and all the cattle; they destroyed it with the edge of the sword. When they had completed their slaughter, the solders lit torches and set fire to the city. That night from their camp in Gilgal, the Israelites watched the crimson flames rising. By morning, Jericho had become a black, smoldering waste land. The Israelites had won their first battle.

Explanation of Jericho's Wall Falling

Some claim the walls were thrown down at an earthquake; that it was timed to occur at the psychological moment when the people shouted. If that be true, there was never an earthquake before or since like it, for only the walls of the city fell flat, with exception of the part where Rahab lived. It was protected by the "scarlet cord" in the window. Not a dwelling house in the city was destroyed when the wall fell flat. This was a command to Joshua; he was to utterly destroy the city and all that was in it—both men and women, children, and all the cattle with the sword. Then he was to burn the city. All this he did. All the silver, gold, brass, and iron vessels were to be put in the treasure of the Lord. See, God did what they could not do. Then, they were to do what they could do.

There are others who claim the walls were thrown down by concussion caused by the blast of the trumpets and the shout of the people. That is, the trumpets and the voices of the people were keyed to the note of the wall causing it to vibrate until it fell. If that were true, why did not the part where Rahab lived not fall?

The True Explanation

We must go back a few verses into the proceeding chapter. There we get the setting for the miracle. In Joshua 5:13, we read that when Joshua was about to besiege Jericho, he was met by a man with a drawn sword in his hand. When Joshua ask him if he was friend or enemy, the reply to Joshua was: "Nay, but captain of the host of the Lord am I come." His command to Joshua was: "Loose thy shoes from off thy feet; for the place whereon thou standeth is holy, and Joshua did so" (Josh. 5:14-15).

The command was the same as to Moses at the burning bush. One cannot help to wonder if it was not the same angel. In the interview that followed, Joshua 6:2-5, Joshua is given instruction in his part of the taking of the city with the aid by the "armies of heaven" under the command of their captain, "the Lord of Host." So, when Joshua and the people fulfilled their part, marching, the priest blowing the trumpets,_ Joshua command to shout. Then, the invisible "angelic army" under the command of their captain, "the Lord of Host," throw down the wall of the city, sparing the part where Rahab's house was.

Confirmation That God's Angels Go to Battle

In 1 Chronicles 14:13-17, the Philistines had spread themselves over the valley; King David inquired to God as to what to do. God said unto him, "Go not up against them; turn away from them, come upon them over against the mulberry trees and it shall be, when thou shalt hear a sound of going in the tops of the mulberry trees, that then thou shalt go out to battle: for God is gone forth before thee to smite the host of the Philistines." Here we see the corporation of an angelic army. Whose presence would be made known by the sound of going marching troops on the top of the mulberry trees.

To the author, it is understood that Joshua was following God's instructions as David did, and the ministering angels did what he could not do.

When time came to destroy Sodom and Gomorrah, two angels were sent to Lot to deliver him. As Elijah lay under a juniper tree, despondent and praying that he might die, an angel brought him bread and water. When Elisha was besieged at Dalton, the angelic host were sent to deliver him, which they did by smiting the enemy with blindness.

When Daniel was thrown in the lions' den, God sent an angel to close the lions' mouth.

After Jesus had fasted forty days, angels came and ministered unto him.

It was angels that delivered Peter from prison.

Psalm 34:7, we read, "The angels of the Lord encamp round about them that fear him, and delivered them."

Some of the most precious words in scripture are spoken by the Devil himself. *Not that he intended it to be so.* With his discussion with God about Job, he said, "Hast thou not made a hedge about his house, and about all that he hath on every side? thou hast blessed the work of his hands and his substance has increase in the land" (Job 1:10).

Thank God for his angelic forces that fight off works of darkness. God has no favorites, and declares that angels will minister to all. While we do not place our faith in angels, we place it in God who rules the angels. As he sent angels to tear down the walls of Jericho, he will send them to tear down walls in our lives. He has not changed; he is the same today as yesterday and will be the same in all the tomorrows.

As For Rahab

Taking the two spies into her house, she took her own life in her hands, not to endanger theirs. As for the spies, it would have gone hard for them, had she not so strangely housed them.

Let us pause here and take a look at Rahab. She was artful, brave, and noble. She received the spies in her door in peace; she let them out at her window by strength; she sent her own townsmen on an idle chase by the river; and she sent the spies to the hills, just because she knew they were spies of Israel.

Listen again to her words: Joshua 2:9-10-11:

9. And she said unto the men, I know that the Lord hath given you the land, and that your terror is fallen upon us, and that all the inhabitants of the land faint because of you.
10. For we have head how the Lord dried up the water of the Red Sea for you, when ye came out of Egypt: and what he did unto the two kings of the Amorites, that were on the other side of Jordan. Sihon and Og, whom thou utterly destroyed.
11. And as soon as we heard those things, our hearts did melt, neither did there remain any more courage in any man, because of you: for the Lord your God, he is God in heaven above and in the earth beneath."

Rahab's words let us know the feelings with which the Canaanites regarded the Israel, in the wilderness. The fame and fear of the Israelites' name had proceeded the people like the wind traveling before the thunderstorm. It was a thing of mystery; a nation that fed from the night and drank from the rock.

Thus from an unlikely source, we are taught the power of faith. Rahab did not know what the word faith meant. Yet the thing itself was in her heart and found expression. Not in words, but in works!

In Hebrews 11:31, you will discover a name there that has been overlooked many times. "By faith the harlot Rahab perished not with them that believed not, when she had received the spies in faith."

Now, being preserved alive, she was left for sometime without the camp to be purified, was in due time incorporated with the Israelites (Matt. 1:5); we find her wife of Salmon, prince of Judah, mother of Boaz, having received Israelites in the name of Israelites, she had a Israelite reward.

From Jericho to Ai

Jericho stood some six miles west of the Jordan River. The ruins of the city, which are oval shaped and covers some thirteen acres, can be seen by travelers today. It elevated about forty feet above the plains and was enclosed by a wall some seven feet thick and about sixteen feet high, made of mud brick. God gave Joshua instruction to destroy everything therein; men, women, children, and cattle. The gold, silver, brass, and iron—these were to be put in the treasure of the Lord. Only Rahab and her family were to be spared. No one was to keep anything for themselves.

In previous study we studied, we saw how the walls fell and the how Rahab was spared. They torched the city. That night from their camp in Gilgal, the Israelites watched the crimson flames rising from Jericho. By morning, Jericho had become a black, smoldering waste land. From the surface, it seemed every instruction had been followed.

Now, moving westward up the mountain from Jericho, their next object was "Ai," a city near Bethel, in the heart of western Palestine.

Highly elated, and perhaps over confident after their decisive victory at Jericho, the Israelites were to taste the bitterness of humiliation defeat. They were utterly defeated. This humiliating experience caused great concern among them.

Led by Joshua, they prostrated themselves before Jehovah. Joshua seemed to blame God for their defeat. But, God commanded Joshua, "Arise and do his duty." There was sin in the camp; there was no time for morning, no time for feeling sorry for self; there was a job to be done.

The Defeat

Contrary to the specific command, none of the valuables of Jericho were to be saved or appropriated, someone was guilty of stealing. Who was it? What was it? Where was the problem?

Now see how God works. The guilty tribe was pointed out. Finally, the guilty one was named. "Achan" of the tribe of Judah. He had hidden in his tent, a rich Oriental robe, two hundred shekels silver, and a bar of gold. When confronted with the crime, Achan confessed to the crime. What was the problem? Achan had taken what belonged to God. He and his family were taken to a valley south of the ruins of Jericho; there, they were stoned to death. A mound of stones was placed above the place and the name "Achor" (troubled) was given to the valley of execution. His tent and all of his possessions were taken and burned. When the sin was removed, the blessings of God returned.

The second battle was much different from the first. This time, Joshua himself led his entire army across the Judean wilderness in the dead of the night. The main part of the army positioned itself across a ravine north of the city. A small force lay ambushed in the valley to the west. At day break, Joshua led his men in a charge against the city. The king and the solders of Ai came out to meet them. They had left the gate to the city open. Meanwhile, the small force circled around the city, marched up the roadway, and stormed through the gate, setting the city on fire. As the women and children ran from their flaming homes into the streets, the Israelites cut them down with their swords and daggers.

Smelling the smoke, the men of Ai looked back. When they saw the flames and black clouds of smoke rising from the city, they panicked and turned back. But now they found they were trapped between the two flanks of the Israelite army. There was no hope of escape.

The Israelite warrior swept into the midst, dealing deathblows to every solder of Ai. The king of Ai was taken alive and brought before Joshua. The Lord's command to Joshua was, "Spare no man's life."

Joshua 8:29: "And the king of Ai he hanged on a tree until eventide, as soon as the sun was down, Joshua commanded that they should take his carcass down from the tree, and cast it at entering of the gate of the city, and raise there a great heap of stones."

Twelve thousand were slain, and all the spoils of the city was given to the people.

At Shechem, there is no record of a great conquest. Later, this area became the core of the nation of Israel. In the time of Israel's judges, it was the home of the dominant tribes of Manasseh and Ephraim. It was a large prosperous settlement at the geographical center of Canaan.

Centuries earlier, the Patriarchs of Israel had made peace with the people of Shechem. Abraham and Jacob had built alters to the Lord near the town. There was an ancient covenant between the people and the family of Jacob. Perhaps for this reason, the Shechemites did not resist the Israelite army. The city and surrounding territory seem to have been incorporated peaceful into Israel.

On to Gibeon

The people of Gibeon, a rich Canaanite town about seven miles southward of Ai, soon heard about Israel's victory and the covenant at Shechem. Hoping to escape the fate of Jericho and Ai, the leaders of Gibeon dressed in tattered clothing, patched sandals, and their bodies covered with dirt and their bread moldy and dry. They approached the Israelites in Gilgal.

Joshua questioned them at length, until he was convinced of their sincerity. Then he made a covenant with them. Together, they swore an oath in the name of the Lord. Three days later, Joshua learned he had been tricked. Ready to do battle, he marched his army to Gibeon. Summoning the elders, angrily he demanded to know why they had deceived him. Their answer, "Because we were told of your servants for a certainty that the Lord your God had commanded Moses to give you all the land and to destroy all inhabitants of the land from before you. So we feared greatly for our lives, because of you did this thing, and now, behold, we are in your hands. Do as it seems good and right in your sight to do to us. Joshua stood good by the covenant he had made with them and spared their lives.

Meanwhile, the kings of five powerful city-states to the south of Gibeon heard of the Israel's league with Gibeon. Combining their armies in full battle form, they marched northward and surrounding Gibeon. Frightened, they sent to Gilgal for aid.

Joshua acted at once. He led his men into the hill country in a night-long trek and surprised the coalition army at dawn. The startled enemy troops fled in dismay. The Israelites and the Gibeonites gave chase and slayed a great number of them. Gradually, the sun was lowering in the west. The darkness would give the enemy refuge.

Joshua 10:17: Joshua spoke to the Lord, asking that the sun and the moon stand still, and they stood still until they took vengeance on their enemies. Those who escaped fled down the hills toward the lower plains near Mahhedah another Canaanite city.

The five enemy kings took refuge in a cave. Joshua gave orders to roll stones upon the mouth of the cave and set men to guard. Then they chased after the enemy, killing everyone before they could reach their cities.

Then he returned back to the cave. On Joshua's orders, the men entered the cave, captured the kings, brought them out before Joshua. One by one, Joshua killed each one of them, had their bodies strung upon trees until night fall, and then had their bodies placed in the cave and sealed with stones.

From here, Joshua takes the whole land. *Joshua* 11:23: "So Joshua took the whole land, according to all that the Lord said unto Moses; and Joshua gave it for an inheritance unto Israel according to the division by tribes and the Lord rested from war."

When the Bible Proved a Computer Correct

Did you know that the space program is busy proving that what has been called a "myth" in the Bible is true? Mr. Harold Hill, president of the Curtis Engine Company in Baltimore, Maryland, and a consultant in the space program relates the following:

I think one of the most amazing things that God has for us today happened recently to our astronauts and space scientists at Green Belt, Maryland. They were checking the position of the sun, moon, and planets out in space where they would be one hundred years and one thousand years from now. We have to know this so we don't send a satellite up and have it bump into something later on in its orbits. We have to lay out the orbits in terms of the life of the satellites and where the planets will be, so the whole thing will not bog down. We ran the computer measurement back and forth centuries, and it came to a halt. The computer stopped and put a red signal, which meant there was something wrong either with the information fed into it or with the results as compared to the standers. They called in the service department to check it out, and they said, "It's perfect" The head of the operations said, "What's wrong?"

"Well, we found there is a day missing in space in elapsed time." They scratched their heads; there was no answer.

One religious fellow on the team said, "You know, onetime when I was in Sunday school, they talked about the sun standing still."

They didn't believe him, but they didn't have any other answer, so they said, "Show us." He got a Bible and went back to the book of Joshua where they found a pretty ridiculous statement for anybody who has common sense. There, they found the Lord saying to Joshua, "Fear them not, for I have delivered them into thy hand: there shall not a man of them stand before thee." Joshua was concerned because he was surrounded by the enemy, and if darkness fell, they would overpower them. So Joshua asked the Lord to make the sun stand still. That's right, the sun stood still and the moon stayed and hastened not to go down about a whole day.

The space men said, "There is the missing day." They checked the computers going back to the time it was written and found it was close, but not close enough. The lapsed time that was missing back in Joshua's day was twenty-three hours and twenty minutes, not a whole day. They read the Bible, and there it was about (approximately) a day.

These little words in the Bible are important. But they were still in trouble because if you cannot account for forty minutes, you will be in trouble in one thousand years from now. Four minutes had to be found because it can be multiplied many times over in orbits. This religious fellow also remembered somewhere else in the Bible where it said the sun went "backward." The space men said he was out of his mind. But he got out the Bible and read the words in 2 Kings. Hezekiah, on his death bed, was visited by the prophet Isaiah who told him he was going to die. Hezekiah asked for a sign as proof. Isaiah said, "Do you want the sun to do ahead ten degrees?"

Hezekiah said, "It is nothing for the sun to go ahead ten degrees, but let the shadow return backward ten degrees." Isaiah spoke to the Lord and the Lord brought the shadow ten degrees "backward." Ten degrees is exactly forty minutes. Twenty-three hours and twenty minutes in Joshua plus forty minutes in 2 Kings make twenty-four hours. The travelers had to log in the logbook as being the missing day in the universe.

This article was published in *The Evening Star*, a newspaper in Spencer, Indiana.

Chapter Twelve

Locating the Tribes

Now the *Promised Land* was finally in the hands of the Israelites. The common task in which all were interested was the division of their new homeland. In the previous chapter, Reuben, Gad, and part of the tribe of Manasseh, upon their request, had been given their territory west of the Jordan River. The remaining tribes were to be given their territory.

Joshua, assisted by Eleazar, the high priest, made arrangements for most of the territory. However, it appears that some of the groups with strong leaders went out and obtained certain locations for themselves.

Caleb reminded Joshua of the promise of Moses secured his claim to Hebron in the southern Palestine territory.

Judah, the strongest of the tribes, was given a large territory which stretched westward from the Dead Sea across the western highlands to the border of Palestine. Much of it was rugged wilderness and barren hill country.

Simeon was given the territory southwest of Judah, which was sandy hill country, whose borders varied from time to time.

Just northwest of Judah, in the hill country sloping down to the sea, the tribe of Dan was first located. However, at a later date, this tribe moved to the far north above the Sea of Galilee. This location became to be know as "The City of Dan."

Benjamin was given the land immediately north of Judah, in the western highlands. This territory was much smaller, but was a choice location. Benjamin's tribe, while not so large in number, was very prominent in national affairs and contributed more than their share of leaders.

North of Benjamin, on the high ridge and extending over east to the Jordan, west to the costal planes, was given to Ephraim and half of the tribe of Manasseh.

The territory known later as the plain of Galilee was assigned to four tribes. Issachar received the fertile plains between Galilee and Samaria. This is the most historic area of Palestine. There is a scene of many important events in both the Old and New Testaments. However, the people of Issachar seem not to have been very prominent in the life of the nation afterward.

Note, in all the assignments, no provision was made for the tribe of Levi. They were the priestly tribe and received no separate province of the land, but were allotted certain cities throughout the tribes. These cities were given to the Levites, either wholly or in part. It is evident that they were not the only places occupied by the priest and that others beside the Levites dwelt in them. The Levitical cities were divided into two classes: those for the priest proper or descendants of Aaron—thirteen in number and all in the tribe of Judah, Simeon, and Benjamin. A remarkable arrangement since the Altar and the Tabernacle were in the tribe of Ephraim. Those for the Levites or subordinate priest, thirty-five in number, divided among the tribes. Thus, there were in all forty-eight Levitical cities. These were so arranged that in each tribe, four cities were assigned to the priest, except in Judah which had more.

Population of the Tribes at the Entrance Into Canaan:-

Tribe	Population
Reuben	174,920
Simeon	88,800
Levi	46,000
Judah	306,000
Dan	257,000
Naphtali	181,600
Gad	162,000
Asher	213,600
Issachar	257,200
Zebulum	242,000
Benjamin	182,400
Manasseh	210,800
Ephraim	130,000

Joshua's Last Days

Some years later, when the Lord had given rest to Israel from all their enemies round about, now Joshua was old. Well, advanced in years, at Shechem, he summoned the elders, the heads of state, and the officers of Israel. Now Joshua speaks to them.

"I am old and well advanced in years, and you have seen all that the Lord your God has done to all those nations for your sake, for it is the Lord your God who fought for you. Therefore, be steadfast to keep and do all that is written in the book of the Law of Moses, and turning aside from it neither to the right hand nor the left. That you may not be mixed with these nations left among you, or make mention of the name of their gods, or swear by them, or serve them, or bow down yourselves to them, but cleave to the Lord your God as you have done to this day."

Joshua then recounted the miracles that the Lord had performed for Israel. He repeated the Lord's promise to Abraham, Isaac, Jacob, and Moses. He reminded them that the Lord had fulfilled his promise to them.

Thus says the Lord, the God of Israel, "I give you a land which you had not labored, and cities which you had not built, and you dwell therein. You eat the fruit of the vineyard and olive yards which you planted not" (Josh. 24:13)

The verse 14: Joshua renews the covenant . . .

Verse 16:_ The people answer, "God forbid that we shall forsake the Lord."

Verse 26: Joshua wrote these words in the book of the law of God. Took a great stone and set it up there under an oak tree, that way by the sanctuary of the Lord.

Then closing he said, "Behold, this stone shall be a witness against us, for it hast heard all the words of the Lord which he spake to us; therefore it shall be a witness again you, lest you deal falsely with your God" (Joshua 24:27).

After these things, Joshua, the son of Nun, the servant of the Lord, died, being a 110 years old.

Joshua 24:31: "And Israel served the Lord all the days of Joshua."

Joshua had served the people with great devotion at a critical time in their history. He followed Israel's great statesman, Moses. It naturally was somewhat overshadowed by him. But his contribution was exceptionally valuable and his own name he stands out as a very remarkable man. As a solder, he was brave and resourceful, showing unusual gifts and strategy. As a civil leader or statesman, he exercised fine foresight and sound wisdom. As a man, he was genuine, courageous, and honorable. In religious matters, he was humble, genuinely faithful to Jehovah, and uncompromising in his efforts to lead his people to wholehearted to the law of Moses.

INDEX

A

Aaron (brother of Moses), 7-8
    death of, 77
    and the establishment of his
        authority, 76
    and the golden calf, 19
    and Moses in the wilderness, 8
    rod of, 9, 61
Abraham (Old Testament patriarch),
    1
Ai, 90-92
Amram (father of Moses), iii, 3
Ark of the Covenant, 61. *See also*
    Tabernacle in the Wilderness

B

Breastplate of Judgment, 66, 69-
    70. *See also* Tabernacle in the
    Wilderness
Burning Bush, 6, 87

C

Canaan, 2, 12, 73, 78-80, 83, 95
    spies sent to, 75

Ceremonial Law, 18
Cherubim, 44, 59, 61, 65

D

Day of Atonement, 51, 64, 71

E

Egypt, 7, 9, 80
    plagues of, 9
Exodus
    2:9, *4*
    4:10, *7*
    12:1-5, *10*
    13:18, *13*
    18:4, *36*
    27:16, *33*
    30:17-18, *38*
    32:25-28, *19*
    32:7, *19*

G

God, 1
    hand of, 4, 6
    Law of, 18

S

Shekinah Glory, 63-65

T

Tabernacle in the Wilderness, 27
  Altar of Incense of, 51-52
  Ark of the Covenant of, 43, 83, 85
  Brazen Altar of, 31, 36, 43
  Court Gate of, *33*
  Golden Candlestick of, 47, 51
  Inner Veil of, 58
  Laver of, 36, 38-39

  Mercy Seat of, 61, 64
  structure of, 43-44
  Table of Shewbread of, 54
ten Commandments, i, 18, 20, 26

W

Word of God, 38-39, 82. *See also*
  Jesus Christ

Z

Zepporah (wife of Moses), 6

Ingram Content Group UK Ltd.
Milton Keynes UK
UKHW010022090623
423139UK00013B/217/J